Reeds and Rushes

Pitch, Buzz, and Hum

Kathleen Burgess, Editor

Reeds and Rushes
Pitch, Buzz, and Hum
Editor: Kathleen S. Burgess

Pudding House Publications
81 Shadymere Lane, Columbus, Ohio 43213
614-986-1881
jen@puddinghouse.com
www.puddinghouse.com

Publisher & Managing Editor: Jennifer Bosveld
Editorial Team: Doug Swisher, Andy Roberts, H. Eugene Bradford
Production Manager: H. Eugene Bradford

ISBN: 978-158998698-5

Reeds and Rushes—Pitch, Buzz, and Hum
Copyright © 2010 Pudding House Publications
All rights reserved

Copyright of individual work reverts to authors. Pudding House retains permission to reprint. No part of the contents of this book may be reproduced by any method or stored in electronic media without written permission of the publisher for the book and the author for individual poems.

FIRST EDITION
Printed and Bound in the United States of America

Cover art: *muses: inspiration*, by Maria Arango, boxwood block woodprint, is used with permission of the artist.

Opinions expressed herein are the views of the authors and do not necessarily reflect the views of the editors.

All Pudding House Publications are archived by The Ohio State University Libraries Special Collections, SUNY/Buffalo Lockwood Library Special Collections, Kent State University Special Collections, Poets House/NYC, private collectors, and the Library at Pudding House Innovative Writers Programs. Books are listed in Bowker/*Books In Print* and may be researched online at www.puddinghouse.com and ordered from Pudding House by phone or U.S. postal mail. Pudding House extends generous discounts to independent bookstores, non-profit organizations, writers' groups, and special events, for bulk purchases.

Cataloging-in-Publication Data:
Main Entry under title *Reeds and Rushes—Pitch, Buzz, and Hum*

2. American Poetry—2010 C.E.   3. Kathleen Burgess   4. Music   5. Flora

Acknowledgments

We appreciate the editors who first published the following poems, some in slightly altered form, in these journals, books, and anthologies:

American Literary Review: "Neanderthal, with Help from Cave and Bear, Invents the Flute," by David Citino. Also in *The News and Other Poems* (University of Notre Dame Press, 2002).
Another Brief Memorial for Wallace Stevens (Pudding House, 2010): "Gardening with Wallace Stevens," by Kathleen S. Burgess.
Chiron Review: "Damnable Instruments," by Kristin Berkey-Abbott.
The Cincinnati Review: "August's Prairie," by Allison Funk.
The Death of the Tenor Sax (Red Weather Press, 1980): "Five Reasons Not to Play the Tenor Saxophone," by Richard Terrill.
Feelings (Anderie Poetry Press, 1992): "Sax," by Marta Ferguson.
Femspec: "Her Baskets," by Sara Littlecrow-Russell.
Flowering Bruno—an illustrated manuscript of dog-besotted poems (XOXOX Press, 2006), "Unmown Spaces," by Charlene Fix.
Fuel: "La Opera," by Allan Douglass Coleman.
Grass Script (Alms House Press, 1991): "Grass Script, Kitty Hawk," by Steve Lautermilch.
The Hudson Review: "Schilfgraben," by James Reiss. Also in *Express* (University of Pittsburgh Press, 1983).
Iron Horse Literary Review: "Last Dream in Perú," by Carolyne Wright. Also in *Greatest Hits, 1975-2001* (Pudding House Publications, 2002).
The Little Piano Book: "Body and Soul," by Robert Samarotto.
Loft and Range, a Poetry Anthology (Pima Press, 2001): "Syrinx," by Nancy Wall.
Nesting Dolls (Pudding House, 2005): "Alum Creek, Late Summer" and "Gigging," by Maggie Smith.
La Petite Zine: "To an Oboe," by Matthew Thorburn. Also in *Subject to Change* (New Issues, 2004).
Pavement Saw: "Arresting Saxophones," by Steve Abbott.
Rosebud: "Because If Things Are Not Carefully Hidden," by Roy Bentley.
Southern Poetry Review: originally published as *"Leaping" (Part I)*, by Julia Older, "Cacoethes scribendi," later appeared in *Hermaphroditus in America* (Appledore Books, 2000) as the prologue.
SyZyGy: "Paul Desmond's Last Date at Symphony Hall, Boston," by Kenneth Salzmann.
Tampa Review: "Flight," by Richard Terrill. Also in *Coming Late to Rachmaninoff* (University of Tampa Press, 2003).
Tea House of the Almighty (Coffee House Press, 2006): "Map Rappin'," by Patricia Smith.
TriQuarterly: "Ginza Samba," by Robert Pinsky. Also in *The Figured Wheel* (The Noonday Press, Farrar, Straus and Giroux, 1996).
Unbidden Angel: "in double life," by Robin Metz.

Contents

Introduction 6
Neanderthal, with Help from Cave and Bear, Invents the Flute **David Citino** 9
Ginza Samba **Robert Pinsky** 10
in double life **Robin Metz** 12
wetlands of lechwe **Spiel** 13
Because If Things Are Not Carefully Hidden **Roy Bentley** 14
La Opera **Allan Douglass Coleman** 15
Poem for Patricia, and Ulli, and Ted **Kathleen S. Burgess** 16
extranjero **Levi Romero** 17
August's Prairie **Allison Funk** 19
Alum Creek, Late Summer **Maggie Smith** 20
cattail club **Spiel** 21
Old Bamboo Fishing Pole **Dick Bakken** 22
Let It Grow **Roy Bentley** 23
Café Foreplay **Dory L. Hudspeth** 24
Kyorei **Carol Lem** 25
The Instrument **Francis L. Richardson** 26
Street Craft **Alexander Levering Kern** 27
Barcelona **Allison A. deFreese** 28
To the Harmonica Players **Rick Smith** 29
Gigging **Maggie Smith** 32
Last Dream in Perú **Carolyne Wright** 33
Grass Script, Kitty Hawk **Steve Lautermilch** 34
The Wetlands Song **Steve Lautermilch** 35
Roadside, Reeds **Rose M. Smith** 36
Papyrus from an Egyptian Tomb **Jeanne Lohmann** 38
Cacoethes scribendi, **Julia Older** 39
Papyrus Wine **Dennis Saleh** 41
Gazing Out Over Lotus **Caroline G. Banks** 43
Kurokami **Carol Lem** 44
Born from Bamboo **Vince Gotera** 46
Reeds **Maureen Tolman Flannery** 46
In the Land of the Snows **Madeline Artenberg** 51
A Space for Light **James A. McGrath** 52
Softstem Bulrush **John Gilgun** 53
My Passover **Kristin Camitta Zimet** 54
A Life **Katharyn Howd Machan** 55
Reeds to Salvation **Hugh Fox** 56
After September 11 **Barbara Crooker** 57
Rifles and Roses **Marianne Poloskey** 58
How We Came to Music **Nancy Sather** 59
A Field in Virginia **Charles Adés Fishman** 60
Gardening with Wallace Stevens **Kathleen S. Burgess** 61

Unmown Spaces **Charlene Fix**	63
chorus no. 1 **Douglas A. Fowler**	64
Miriam **J.E. Robinson**	65
Autopsy **Jennifer Bosveld**	66
Pathétique **Gina M. Tabasso**	67
The Music We Play **Leonard Orr**	68
Undated Valentine **Tony D'Arpino**	69
Drinking Scene on an Attic Vase **Danny di Crispino**	70
Syrinx **NancyWall**	71
Sharette dedicates a song to her daughter, conceived by a rape, and to her son-in-law on their wedding day. **Danny di Crispino**	72
Damnable Instruments **Kristin Berkey-Abbott**	74
Schilfgraben **James Reiss**	75
Her Baskets **Sara Littlecrow-Russell**	76
Yellow Corn Woman's Third Daughter **Sarah Brown Weitzman**	77
Rowing Across Wild Rice Lake **Sheryl L. Nelms**	78
Sky of Reeds **James A. McGrath**	79
A Disquisition upon Thatch on the Way to Jane Austen's **Lynn Veach Sadler**	80
Electronic Clarinet: A Lament **Sharon Scholl**	82
Linn Seeks the Musings of Music **Daniel M. Gallik**	83
Woodwinds **Sherman Pearl**	84
Paul Desmond's Last Date at Symphony Hall, Boston **Kenneth Salzmann**	85
Phragmites' Foe **George Held**	86
What Goes in by the Hand Goes out by the Hand **Jen Karetnick**	87
Driftwood **Vanessa Kittle**	88
Bamboo **Elizabeth Ann James**	89
Five Reasons Not to Play the Tenor Saxophone **Richard Terrill**	90
To an Oboe **Matthew Thorburn**	91
Hautbois and the Night Visitors **Donna Pucciani**	92
In Memory **Paula Chertok**	93
Sax **Marta Ferguson**	94
Body and Soul **Robert Samarotto**	95
Arresting Saxophones **Steve Abbott**	96
Flight **Richard Terrill**	98
Listening to Coltrane's Blues **David Williams**	100
Map Rappin' **Patricia Smith**	101
Contributor Notes	104

Introduction

Looking at the garden bamboo and large grasses bent low by snow, before my husband and I go walking past corn fields and through a small forest along North Fork, I'm thinking about small creatures that might be concealed in grass, cattails, and horsetail reeds along the trail. I'm also reflecting on all that's led to the creation of this anthology, *Reeds and Rushes—Pitch, Buzz, and Hum*.

As a young woman I hitchhiked to South America and met regional musicians, listened to their music, and collected their hand-crafted instruments. As a flutist and music teacher for students of all ages, I've shared these instruments with thousands. A passionate listener, reader, and writer, I also study politics, world cultures, art, and pre-Columbian history. So, when Jennifer Bosveld asked me to join the Pudding House editorial team and to initiate a project, perhaps an anthology, I decided the theme of reeds, rushes, and their extended plant families would allow me to work with major interests and concerns as I collected poetry to fill this book.

Grasses. Rushes. Reeds. Wherever we find them growing, we notice their sounds in wind: rapid vibrations that *shush*, and sometimes emit tones which may have inspired the first woodwind instruments. The poems that follow focus on these plants. They shelter animals and people alive or dead in wetlands, prairies, lakes, and forests over five continents. They give birth to the first humans. We use them to roof homes, and to serve as a floating ground on which to live. They enable us to travel in reed boats. Egyptians wrote on sliced and beaten papyrus reeds (the first "paper") in 3500 B.C.E. They drank papyrus wine. Rush baskets protect what is precious, even a Biblical baby.

Reeds sustain our rituals and connect us. They suggest names for indigenous people. From reeds men weave roses and crosses for tourists near Savannah's old slave market. Cattails initiate members of a boys' secret club as they decide to enlarge their group. Grass covers the burial place of assassinated Spanish poet Federico Garcia Lorca, and grass will one day cover many of us, no matter who wins which wars waged for peace.

Composer Joan La Barbara has said voice is the original instrument. Hearing, our first sense, develops between 20 and 30 weeks of gestation. A fetus recognizes parental voices speaking, reading, and singing during the third trimester. Because early, intimate exposure to music causes a rich branching of brain receptors (dendrites) that optimize brain growth in linguistic, mathematical, musical, and other learning areas, as well as essential emotional responsiveness, we cannot overstate the importance of music.

The voice—two vocal folds within a larynx—though mechanically more complex, resembles a double-reed instrument. Air opens vocal folds, which respond by closing and opening rapidly. The faster the air, the higher the pitch; conversely, the slower the air, the lower the pitch. Exceptional coloratura soprano voices may reach high notes above 1100 hertz (Hz), or 1100 vibrations per second, while "Russian bass" or basso profundos may achieve lows below 82 Hz.

After voice, percussion instruments, then woodwind instruments were created. With air reeds (flutes and recorders), air blown across an edge creates sounds. Single-bladed clarinets and saxophones vibrate when their shaped reeds are blown into motion against a mouthpiece. The double reeds of oboes and bassoons vibrate against each other. From the contrabassoon which plays the lowest note, 29 Hz, in an orchestra of common instruments, to the piccolo with its highest note, 4096 Hz, woodwinds, like voices, cover a strikingly wide range of frequencies (determining pitches) and a complementary emotional range.

Music is often called the language of emotions, with the potential for universal understanding. So recognizable is a woodwind's timbre, or characteristic sound, that hearing an instrument may evoke emotions we have previously identified with it. For thousands of years, over every inhabited continent, reeds have channeled breath into emotional displays whether simple, earnest, religious, playful, wicked, virtuosic, or other states. And we create music, no matter how dangerous or subversive the act.

David Citino's "Neanderthal, with Help from Cave and Bear, Invents the Flute" begins the anthology in Slovenia over 40,000 years ago as "the first flute / the closer-to-beastly unkin of us / worked, out of starless dark, / the melodies of bear, / and birds lifting off at dawn. The cave / is a flute, the skull is a flute...." From this bear bone flute, the earliest known woodwind, to Adolph Sax's latecomer, to recent electronic adaptations, reeds stimulate, provoke, and connect us.

I thank Jennifer Bosveld for enabling and encouraging this project, and I thank the poets, both distinguished and gifted new voices, for their generous and enthusiastic sharing with Pudding House and now with you. Read these poems aloud. Reeds, rushes, grasses, the human voice, the spirit of music resound through this collection, rooting in stone, curling through bone, shooting up through decay, myth, memory, and meditation, to leaf into life, into breath, into the body's vibrant listening.

Kathleen S. Burgess

David Citino

Neanderthal, with Help from Cave and Bear, Invents the Flute

In the dark cave of Slovenia,
    40,000 years of utter silence.
No one to lift this leg bone of bear.

Two finger-holes punched through
    to take the mortal breath away,
end open to let out the skein

of tones closer to human moan
    than human moan, hoot of moon
wind-honed, horned, fervid scents,

fevered puddles of bison blood, beak
    and breath of Gray Father, steam
of Mother Milk. We didn't know

Neanderthals had an ear.
    We didn't know they beatified
their dead with color. In petal,

pistil, stamen they invented
    prayer, and on the first flute
the closer-to-beastly unkin of us

worked, out of starless dark,
    the melodies of bear, and birds
lifting off at dawn. The cave

is a flute, the skull is a flute
    for wish to move through, true,
eye and nose hole waiting for

the skill to finger out our voices.
    From the bones of our parents
we tease out the music of us.

Robert Pinsky

Ginza Samba

A monosyllabic European called Sax
Invents a horn, walla whirledy wah, a kind of twisted
Brazen clarinet, but with its column of vibrating
Air shaped not in a cylinder but in a cone
Widening ever outward and bawaah spouting
Infinitely upward through an upturned
Swollen golden bell rimmed
Like a gloxinia flowering
In Sax's Belgian imagination

And in the unfathomable matrix
Of mothers and fathers as a genius graven
Humming into the cells of the body
Or cupped in the resonating grail
Of memory changed and exchanged
As in the trading of brasses,
Pearls and ivory, calicos and slaves,
Laborers and girls, two

Cousins in a royal family
Of Niger known as the Birds or Hawks.
In Christendom one cousin's child
Becomes a "favorite negro" ennobled
By decree of the Czar and founds
A great family, a line of generals,
Dandies and courtiers including the poet
Pushkin, killed in a duel concerning
His wife's honor, while the other cousin sails

In the belly of a slaveship to the port
Of Baltimore where she is raped
And dies in childbirth, but the infant
Will marry a Seminole and in the next
Chorus of time their child fathers
A great Hawk or Bird, with many followers
Among them this great-grandchild of the Jewish
Manager of a Pushkin estate, blowing

His American breath out into the wiggly
Tune uncurling its triplets and sixteenths—the Ginza
Samba of breath and brass, the reed
Vibrating as a valve, the aether, the unimaginable
Wires and circuits of an ingenious box
Here in my room in this house built
A hundred years ago while I was elsewhere.

It is like falling in love, the atavistic
Imperative of some one
Voice or face—the skill, the copper filament,
The golden bellyful of notes twirling through
Their invisible element from
Rio to Tokyo and back again gathering
Speed in the variations as they tunnel
The twin haunted labyrinths of stirrup
And anvil echoing here in the hearkening
Instrument of my skull.

Robin Metz

in double life

this duskiness
there was about you
that for months I have neglected
like a portrait left behind in other summers'
tears and render only in a dream this now and then
all morning in the memory and tremor of the dream
this duskiness this warmth of prelude scent and loam enfolding
cascade hair in swales of dream mahogany and sheen veneers
the oboe song of it the viol hollows of the body musk
of it in lullaby and zither drowse this duskiness
that I remember now all morning now
of you this rhapsody of mystery
I loved in song and life
on earth and you
and most this
duskiness

wetlands of lechwe

how can i swallow this lump
this reality that my extraordinary life in africa
is drawing to a close
as i sit atop kabwibwe hill
these orange clouds glow like hot coals
then turn to black sky and white rain
so reminiscent of the plains of colorado
where i will return
this vast overview of the woodlands
spattered with butterflies and wild orchids
lilies and glads and peculiar flowers
exotic beyond my dreams
the silly *go-away* birds
and a tree full of weavers' complex nests
housing this year's crop of new babies
and the green frog's frothy meringue
overhanging a puddle of water
awaiting the drop of its young
giant edible mushrooms are poking their heads
out of the ground amid brilliant green grasses
that house ticks and shortly they will be too tall
for safe wandering because of snakes and hidden beasties
and beyond all this: the panorama of the great flood flats
the unforgettable sight of the rare kafue lechwe in vast herds
so gracefully leaping among termite mounds
and the pliant reeds of the rainy season
like a living sea of lithesome horns
only to disappear
as i will soon
when the dry season comes

Roy Bentley

Because If Things Are Not Carefully Hidden

They shot the poet Federico Garcia Lorca
on a hillside flecked with olive trees,
in the company of a pair of bullfighters
and a schoolteacher. The sun had not risen
when Lorca and his companions heard the click of rifles.[3]
Grave diggers, blackly obedient, went to work
in the pre-dawn, a lead man deciding depth
and the disposition of certain tree roots.

Years later, one of the diggers says the order
shivered the spine. He recalls the officer who
gave it chewed a reedy stalk of grass to pulp
and that the marathon work proceeded slowly:
"because if things are not carefully hidden…"
He says the last shovelfuls of Spanish earth
were light-struck, there being no words for
finish this grave that might as well be yours.

---

[3] Leslie Stainton, *Lorca: A Dream of Life* (NYC: Farrar, Straus, Giroux, 1999), 454.

Allan Douglass Coleman

La Opera

Sitting below Zapata's bullet,
six blocks off the *Zócalo*—
dark chamber of the universal heart,
where the poor cut reeds forever
for their shrilling flutes and beat
the drums of this pulsing world

(Mexico City, September 1996)

Kathleen S. Burgess

Poem for Patricia, and Ulli, and Ted

The shaman rested in the shadow of St. Thomas Church
after the long parade, after shouldering a palanquin,

its heavy wooden saint painted and dressed in satin
sewn with sequins, mirrors, gaudy fringe, wooden eyes

glazed beneath a Guatemalan sun. One of the cofradía
brotherhood who tend the saints, he wouldn't bargain,

so I paid his asking for a kind of medieval keyless oboe,
a handmade chirimía, played in consort with double-headed

drums of log and goatskin at the Dance of the Conquistadors
and sacred festivals on Chichicastenango's market days.

Back at the pensión near Lago Atitlán, our friends found
my attempts at playing crude triangular double reeds so

discordant and unpleasant, I left to find some other place
to practice. I walked up a path until forest became a swamp.

My eyes blurred with tales of quicksand, alligators, snakes,
and painful deaths. I halted. Ten eyes appraised me.

Bald red heads and necks turned above white collars
as though the five masked, not as a sanitation crew, but as

nosferatu, priests, or Nixons. Hunch-backed they pivoted
and opened large dark wings like cloaks, flight feathers wide

in V-for-Victory salutes. The shifting zopilotes could only hiss
without syrinx, a larynx, a sounding box to give them voice.

In the stench of carrion and sulfurous water, they recycled
death. I blew for them to take my song because it was all I had:

song of wounding, song of war, song of the dispossessed.

Levi Romero

extranjero

and what are the names
in the envelopes that're
stuck still further inside the
bigger envelope?

and whose face
name
sound of voice

will each one belong to
who, who, is who?

the click of china

the soft touch of pen
red ink

the bird's chatter

it is in the blood

and the sameness

ritual

this old familiar town feeling to me strange

where are Orlando, Chris,
and Melvin, the R.D.T. boys
los vatos de Ranchos

all that then
all those other years
where?

the open flap, unlicked envelope
of the new and the now

takes its immediacy
and I've been having visions

cemetery crosses
off the road to El Prado

edgeworn headstones
deep blue sky, chamisa
the cemetery near Talpa

is that what the famed Taos artists felt
when they first came here

the familiar strange?

Tiwa
Castellano
Coyote

sharp, ancient,
prickling barbed-wire
a rusted bolt latch

gnarled, twisted, wire wrapped
around the gate post

at breakfast this morning strangers sat together
told stories
shared bread

it might've been stranger still
to not partake

personal observations, thoughts
kept to the self
the edges softened

the years, history
piled like padded mounds of earth
and prayer

ragweed growing
amidst the flowering
graveyards

Allison Funk

August's Prairie

The tall grass is flattened where they bedded down.
In the morning it shines like a cat
that has licked itself clean.

The fawn and her mother lay there all night.
Now they are gone, just the ghosts
of their bodies remain.

The prairie they've disappeared into is waking up also.

Still, little moves but my shadow along the mown path,

and, in the highest branches of the white poplar,
the leaves as busy as waves turning over—
silver, then dark green again.

Later the wind will come up, making the whole field look tidal,

making everything living bow down:
the Joe-Pye Weed, Queen of the Prairie,
the coneflowers locals call Lazy Susans.

Already the bluestem taller than I am
sways a little on its stalks.

At the compass plant
I stop to consider my direction.

But what for?

The Indian grass doesn't worry its golden head
over where it is going.
It counts on a good breeze by afternoon.

Its yellow anthers looking so like saffron
are just waiting.

Believe it,
pollen can blow anywhere.

Most likely, though, it will stay close to home.
Where it started, it will start again.

Maggie Smith

Alum Creek, Late Summer

The last, desperate days of August are burnished.
At twilight on Plumb Road, a bloody doe
slumps, twitching, in the soft shoulder.
Headlights flash in her blank eye and whiten
her hooves, each curve of bone a crescent moon.
Hawks slip their haggard bodies into pines
and silver maples. I may never leave Ohio.
Its burrs and rusted grass conspire to keep me.
There is always blood in the reeds off Plumb,
always a doe's eye glazed in moonlight.
The hawks' scalloped wings taken wholly
into the dark are keys in a lock. I feel a hand
opening in my chest. It is almost unbearable.

cattail club

three years in a row
we been fighting about it
whether gregorio can join our club
up at the cattails
cause roger didn't want no spics in it

then last october
greg's old man took him hunting
let him help skin a eight point buck he shot
then ride on the roof of his jeep cherokee
into town
with the rack sticking up between his legs

so we're meeting at the big ditch
this saturday to let blood
me and mark, david, mikey, gordon, roger,
and this time, gregorio,
and we'll slit our forefingers
on the cattail leaves
and share brother blood with a spic
for the first time
since we made the cattail club

Dick Bakken

Old Bamboo Fishing Pole

Who we're bothered by
is that old gummer unsnagging the hook
from what's in his wasted hand. Not anything
he could swallow. Just what he's reeled
from this drizzletown slough. A squashed yellow bush
broad as his palm, stickers fanning out
like bones of something finished
long ago. I could leap
all over his puddle. He raises up the catch
for his blue eye
toward our great dim burst of light.
His back almost unbends.
You tell me what falls over his face.
He can lay down the pole.
He can go home.
Supper will be waiting.

Roy Bentley

Let It Grow

I remember driving somewhere in my Firebird
with my friend Butch Thompson riding shotgun
and we were listening to *461 Ocean Boulevard*
by Eric Clapton. The night was black, no moon;
cornfields on both sides of the road were part of
a middle-of-nowhere Illinois dark. From Detroit,
a sucker for the Motown Sound, Stevie Wonder,
he was no fan of Eric Clapton, didn't get the whole
Derek & the Dominos thing. Said, joking, "Who
sings 'let it grow' unless he's got a small cock?"
I tried to look his direction, but I had the Firebird
floored, the accelerator pedal flat to the carpet,
and we were both blind-wrecked on Thai stick,
an opium-laced reed you smoked then, so I kept
my eyes on the headlight threads and white line.
I was centering the white line in the dead middle
of the car's hood because 140 doesn't allow
for mistakes. I'd been busting to wind out
that 350 V-8: "do it to it," as they said in 1974.
Maybe Butch was scared and making small talk
to keep from pissing himself, but he didn't seem
scared, saying, "yeah, yeah" over the engine-roar.
Looking back, at 53, I get a shiver when I think
all it would have taken was one car, one bored
farm-kid in a wired-together fast car of his own,
and giddyup. I thought then, if I thought at all,
*What the hell difference does it make? Death
is going to hit us head-on anyway, right?* Butch
Thompson survived riding with me that night,
though he never appreciated Old Slowhand's
dictum to plant your love in whatever corner
of Nowhere blooms before you, is there and gone,
so absolutely gone it smacks of your own end,
races at you like the blackest asphalt; an end
you do well to toss off with a "yeah, yeah."

Dory L. Hudspeth

Café Foreplay

How carefully over
and over the harmonica
player kisses
a napkin watching
that red impression
fade between each kiss
before she plays the blues.

Carol Lem

Kyorei

    (Empty Bell)

I hear sensei's voice,
"Be in the space at the end of a phrase
before moving on."

With the shakuhachi
poised at my lips,
I sit alone in my small room
above a busy boulevard
as though in a temple,
the wind through the pines trees
and an empty bell above.

"Blow that sound," I hear.
But chatter runs through like a restless
child or an unanswered memo.
The phone rings, a leg twitches.

"It's the echo as it fades away,"
so I stay on my zafu, while
the clapper in my head slows down,
words drift like falling leaves
to where I am inside the notes.
In this space, breath rises,
ready for the next phrase,
and lets go.
In this momentary place, I hear
the voice of silence.

Not quite prayer nor trance
but some interior chant
calling me *home*.
Though I don't know what it is,
when I'm *there*, it has to
take me in.

    (*sensei*, teacher; *shakuhachi*, Japanese bamboo flute; *zafu*, meditation pillow)

Francis L. Richardson

The Instrument

A shape of breath;
A ladder for sound, whose detachable rungs
Are fingers; an old thought articulate in
A new, wood throat.

The thought is wondering Haydn's, the breath
Is mine, but no human cry only
Is so pure.

This is the voice of the pear tree
Which did not know that it lived.

Alexander Levering Kern

Street Craft

In the fashionable squares of Savannah
the live oaks grow mossy dreadlocks
and watch.
From reeds and palm leaves, old homeless men
weave crosses and roses for tourists
who park their cars above the forgotten slave market,
blind to its signs.
In weaving their reeds, the men spit,
prick fingers, and mutter memory.
They listen long for the Low Country drums
across the waters, through the rice paddies
and groaning rushes.
Beyond the Sea Islands the ancestors wait,
biding their time.
The men finish their work
with a fierce tearing of grass,
then nod toward nightfall.
In the dark they wait for the sign
to fly away home.

Allison A. deFreese

Barcelona

City-colored pigeons
scatter the window sills.

A canary hops staccato
to the sides of its cage.

The girl at the flower market
rolls baby's breath and snapdragons
in green paper

pieces of me catching as I walk—
in windows, in storefront mirrors:
my nose, an ear and hair,
my swinging arm. I stop at a café
to order *vino del verano*. A pig's leg
is propped on the counter, hoof
pointed high as a dance slipper.

Outside an old man lifts a bent harmonica to his lips
holds it there, a weathered silver bone.
His cardboard sign says he is hungry,
in front of him a cup for coins.

He weaves air into a clear broth of sound
with here and there a dab of potato
or carrot in it.
He weaves the dry air
of the whole tired city in and out of his mouth.

Rick Smith

To the Harmonica Players

We play harmonica because we have to. We are the bastard sons of the blues. I was born on the very same day that Charlie Christian died and I always want to be that close to that sound. His bus was leaving when mine was pulling in. My grandfather played guitar, too. But he drank too much and left my grandma with just an old amp and a baby girl. My grandma wouldn't talk about it. Mom says he was a good-looking man, a Cherokee from the Upper Peninsula. That's about all she knows except they got $14 for the amp at a yard sale.

I

(What We Do)

A player will cup the harp
in hands locked and hinged.
Breath has heat and propeller blades of pure muscle
carve the tone. The sound waves will
make temperature change,
make neon shimmer and buzz.
We explore the most primal metaphysics:

> God and the Devil
> in hot debate
> about sin and temptation,
> glory and faith.
> The Lord's got smart money
> on Job.
> Devil says, "go ahead, lay it down,
> ten-to-one
> the farm boy folds."

Tonight in the jaw and the chest,
in the lips, tongue and throat
there is a beating
and some door opens
before I knock.

We stand strong and keep company with
the ghosts of Charlie Christian, Les Paul,
Django and Robert Johnson
until a muddy glow appears
over Texas
until Chicago shines
like a fool
in love.

II

(Walter Jacobs/You Better Watch Yourself)

upstairs in a boarder's room,
New Hope, Pennsylvania, 1958,
a volcanic presence
irresistible and reckless,
a wild ride on the Mississippi sax
from outer space

a library in Iowa City, 1968,
headlines in a French jazz
rag: "Petit Walter est Mort."

Walter, you better watch yourself,
look at your shredded face:
solos too close to the sun
like your knife fights:
about passion, longing, scar tissue.
You whisper Juke, Juko, Jukare
into a mad dog's ear,
and
when you play, we stop breathing,
Walter,
you are dangerous.

III

(It's always nine below zero at 3 o'clock in the afternoon)

So each day, at noon, Sonny Boy used to hit the airwaves over Arkansas. He sucked his desperate lyric from a harp shell like he was taking Communion. The hoarse whisper of a man hurting from profound thirst. Sonny Boy II was Shaky Tim's favorite but Sonny was not the best choice to save him or to invite introspection. Still, Tim couldn't lie to himself when he broke into "Help Me" or ran through the outtakes and forbidden passages of "Little Village." There is no room for lying in those tunes. Otherwise, if Tim went into a confession box, he'd have to pack a lunch. So, he never went there. He rolled through the ambiguous teachings of his broken brother and his wine soaked Dad, both preachers. He wasn't with the church; he found his comfort in Sonny Boy. He learned to work the harmonica, make it growl in the lower registers so there was an edge to it. If you read Dante, you know that where you lose the thread that's where you make your bed and Tim lost it somewhere in the 13th Canto; when he went down, he went down hard and he stayed down like a root ball. He died in the bathroom, on cool tile, in a space that barely accommodated his fallen frame. He was dead before he hit the floor. The report said "heart failure" but that was a metaphor and everybody but Shaky's mom knew exactly what it meant. Shaky Tim is buried 6 feet beneath the cliffs at Carpintería with a C harp at his chest. The wind is almost finished forgetting about him; it's the wind has the last word.

Maggie Smith

Gigging

Near the tracks where freighters hauled
West Virginia coal, a boy gigged frogs
in summer darkness with his grandmother
and great aunt. Waist-deep in the reeds,
the women gathered their skirts above
brackish water. One trained a flashlight
on the boy as he forked each slick,
moon-pale belly. The other carried
the sloshing bucket, where the frogs
cured in brine on the back porch.

The next day, the women severed
the legs, floured them, and laid them
in a skillet with oil; the boy watched
as they jerked and trembled.
This was southern Ohio in the '50s.
He would remember this reflex
in the crackling oil. How his breath sang
low across the mouths of soda bottles.
After supper, how nothing but porch light
hummed in the emptied bucket.

Carolyne Wright

Last Dream in Perú

    Lake Titicaca

It was my job
to mimic the crane's cry
as my friends and I skiffed
through the estuary reeds.
But how could I, unless my life
beat in the heart of the bird
and looked through his eye?
My own name was all
I could call.

As they rowed, my friends told me
how, under the floors of their cabins,
they'd excavated old stone walls
whose joints were still
as mortarless and smooth as faces
without memories or dreams.

All I meant to say went quiet.
Real cranes cried
above the thin wind.

It was time to turn back
to land. Before we reached
the shore, I'd have to find
an opening in the water
that fit my speech,
and whisper my name in it
before the lake closed over
and sank it like a stone.

    With thanks to Jon Lang

Steve Lautermilch

Grass Script, Kitty Hawk

All morning's surf you flew,
over the sea, over the sound,
every time the wind picked up
your wings beat down,

tracing the arcs of a circle
whose center was the blossom
of your heart. By afternoon
you had written your name.

By evening your dance turned to stone.
Now under the umbrella of pearling
dark I stand and am still.

Flown beauty
comes down to this
night, lost words, and silence.

Steve Lautermilch

The Wetlands Song

What can I bring to you, with empty
pockets and giveaway heart? There are the great rolling clouds
that pillow the mountaintops and bed down the valleys
and are so light of touch, and delicate, they feather tick the sun
and pillow the moon and neither flinch nor burn.

But you know the clouds, how they change,
come and go and bring the rain. Yes, there is the rain
of April and May, the long, hard pours of summer,
and the blowing snow and blinding ice that shake down and collar the trees
and leave them crazed and sainted for their shimmering.

Yet rain is yours already, and the slow burning grasses of the shore
that sing and bend and are broken and return. Maybe
I could give you one of these,
a word, say, to plant and tend and grow like a root, so that when you read
its letters, call its name, you become its sun, its moon, its light rain.

The riddle of the grasses. So on this day of cloud and wave, wind
and slow silences, reading these lines, whispering pauses,
like a sea you breathe
and with the music of your breathing
are their truth, their beauty, and their heart.

Rose M. Smith

Roadside, Reeds

I cannot write this poem. It waves
in fronds of pampas grass along lakeside roads,
bows constantly to winds of change,
turns colors with the seasons—
sprays of cloud feather riding
crests of slender reeds,
clusters of smoke seed crowning
dormant shoots, riding, rigid through
biting winter winds.
One never knows quite which picture will
spring from its jagged lines.

It calls again in palm and stubborn fern,
pushes up through grasses in the wet,
sprouts heads of cinnamon—dark harbingers
of leaves pushing toward life-promise
moments before leaving us. Full of holes,
it renders haunting flute calls
at the hands of seated listeners
fingering its smooth sides
with slow, responsive vision.

We think we know this poem, think
we've seen its stanzas often enough
to paint it in dry syllable on pages
of a journal some soul after us will read,
straight shoots lingering long after
life and flow have left in dusty annals.
Open-hearted expression of a constant
windswept dance
trapped in edge and periphery
or a single round shoot trained to
stand and curl, bow and vacillate—
a water-vase sentinel set in our paths
to summon luck and venture.

A more focused eye will find revelation
in its many-ness: Innumerable hands
raised, waving, in a field of all their brothers,
a ditch, a stream.
It pushes in without invitation,
teaches us, in the middle of upright,
the ability to bend.

Jeanne Lohmann

Papyrus from an Egyptian Tomb

> *There is papyrus by the river, and rushes for light,*
> *and the goose only flies overhead, ages before*
> *the studious are born or letters invented*
> —Henry David Thoreau
> *A Week on the Concord and Merrimac Rivers*

we ask the symbols to bless us:
the corded grain and the sun
over water, the goose

forever in flight, this procession
of lifting and kneeling, hieroglyphs
like music I will never understand,

small mysterious marks
telling of children
and a drunken man in his sleep

> *here the papyrus*
> *begins to tatter*
> *the rest is lost...*

Julia Older

Cacoethes scribendi,

this passionate desire to write
and be written, to trap print
like insects in amber
and make plain the prophecies
that determine our birth before we are born.

"What I have written, I have written:"
on stones on caves on graves,
on brothel and tavern walls
with ochre and the wingless cochineal,
with bulrush and flint chisel on monolithic stone.
I have written the wedged serif,
the snake and eagle, the hieroglyph
with its watery S's, the X
of the crossroads
scratched on talus
by the dagger of nomads
before moving on.

I have set my tongue
in the curve of the cursive
from a linear sharpness
to the circular reed
plucked from the air
to embellish papyrus
unrolled by the King,
signed with his signet,
and sealed in gold
while the ignorant peasant
gives up his thumb print
distinct as the whorl
of a singular shell, literate only
in famine, earthquake and flood.

"What I have written, I have written:"
my hand setting down
illumined *Hours*
of the bird and the beaste
in strokes of light,
my hand setting down
type of clay, of tin, of lead
and then not set at all,
but fed. Unmoving face.
A microcosmic chip
of earth crust
uniting the links
from A to B to C.

And so we sit
before the circuit
(reed uncut, sighing).
The screen retrieves
the processed word,
leaves behind
the King, the Poet
the ruminating Philosopher.
The abstract leap of the ideogram
is put to sleep.

The word devolves
as information
without encumbrance
of intuition
or imagination,
without the dance
of fingertips on the pen.
Without within.

Dennis Saleh

Papyrus Wine

1.

Paper is very godly for it is white
and full of promise Paper
was next to godliness in the
first days of the age of pages
when there was greater
understanding of its whiteness
What better for writing down
directions to the desert or to gods
Where better news of paper
than in the past The very first
words were the gods' thoughts
given man to know the glory
of worship and the breath of
providence is upon each page

2.

The papyrus is the Lord God's mirror
and the words upon it are in His image
The song of paper the scribes chant
unrolling sheets and cat whisker quills
in Byblos and Tyre and Sidon is His
praise thanksgiving for the miracle
of the paper the lamp of the sun
and the favor of He who makes all
things as a scroll before the ink
Osiris be Osiris Come and sit beside us
Rhyme with the papyrus make it sing
Fill thou page of white this day

3.

And in the shadow of the Nile
the reeds joyous with ten thousand
thoughts of fruition in the seed
And in the night priests blinded
by vapors in the hidden rite
ferment a milksap that
pours whiter than at noon
than a hundred palace columns
than the moon upon the sands
In the false hour O White
strengthen and reprove us
In the peace of paper is the dawn

Caroline G. Banks

Gazing Out Over Lotus

Chou Tun-i stares out
over the lotus pond
from his summer retreat
raised up on stilts
over the water's edge.
Hiding from the sun
under the ornate shelter's
roof and blinds,
he sits for hours at his desk,
the paper, brushes, and ink
carefully arranged before him.
Lost in reverie
he does not see
the fisherman in his simple houseboat
moored nearby in the bamboo reeds,
his foot dangling in the water
while he plays his flute.

I want Chou Tun-i
to push back his chair,
stand up and turn away
from the paper, brushes and ink,
to step down from his retreat
and feel the muck and slime
of the long lotus roots
under his feet.

I want this for myself.

(based on "Chou Tun-i Gazing Out Over Lotus"
by Liu Chun, China, ©1500)

Carol Lem

Kurokami

    (Black Hair)

Playing *Kurokami*
on my shakuhachi and thinking
of that Japanese poem, "My hair
was loose on the pillow at night,"
I too am alone, remembering
how once my black hair
tied him in my heart, hair
he never touched. Gray strands
fall to the floor without grief.
Only the train groans
in the still night.

With my bamboo voice, I call
back the ghosts of ancestral tales:
the woman, her prince,
his house, that cursed night
of blooming moon flowers.
Yugao echoes another fall,
twenty-two years ago, Halloween,
when Death tricked its way
across our threshold.
The last song cries out for you.

The tune of autumn, *Aki No Shirabe*,
is a leaf on the river
drifting toward an unknown dwelling.
This story depicts the longing
that love brings when it is out of reach.
And the young woman, listening
for her song by the window, waits.

This flute, this bamboo raft,
keeps me afloat between these lives
I lived once and survived.

So why on this autumn night
in October am I blowing these old tunes
again? How are these leaves
shaping a different story,
now that other strands of gray
float on my pillow?

Vince Gotera

Born from Bamboo

    In remembrance of my paternal grandmother,
    whom we called Nanay (Tagalog for *mother*)

"Gray-haired man with three summer-blue eyes,"
said Nanay. Fructuosa Gotera, her name: *fruitful*,
fertile. "That was Bathala, god of the skies."

My father, just four, looked up at his mother's smile.
Slim as bamboo, she went on: "Aman Sinaya,
goddess of the sea, had green eyes, like emerald.

Both gods tried to outdo each other every day.
Thunder and lightning. Tidal waves and typhoons.
Aman Sinaya's monsoons raked the sky.

Bathala hurled boulders—" "No, whole mountains!"
said my father, eyes glimmering. "Yes, Martin . . .
mountains! into the sea, creating our islands,

all seven thousand. Meanwhile, caught between
the two realms of heaven and ocean, the northeast
wind Amihan had had enough. She took on

the shape of a bird, with indigo feathers and feet.
She shuttled back and forth, with dainty *alimasag*
crabs, tiger prawns in tamarind, starfish,

anemone flowers, from the wavelets up to Bathala,
then down with shooting stars, planets' rings, moons
for Aman Sinaya to braid in her jade-tinged hair.

With gifts and sweets, letters bathed in perfume,
the bird enticed Aman Sinaya and Bathala
to be friends—" "No," said Martin, "wife and husband!"

"Maybe, my son," Nanay laughed. "In his joy, Bathala
flew over the sea and cast not rocks but his seed
into the Mindanao Deep. From Aman Sinaya's

seabed sprang a gigantic bamboo reed,
swaying between sky and water." Nanay's hand,
upheld in front of my father, danced a sweet

fandango in the air. "One day, Amihan,
now a huge hawk, soared in circles
round the sky-high bamboo, spiraling down

until she stopped, hovered. Did she hear calls
from within the reed? *Help us, Princess of the Air!*
Small *kulintang* gongs. Voices in madrigal.

Amihan pecked the bamboo, laying bare
a tiny space, a womb in the reed. Inside,
the first humans: brown eyes and skin, black hair.

Amihan named the woman Maganda—
beautiful. The man she called Malakas—
strong. Inviting them onto her back, the bird

ferried the two humans through glorious clouds
to the northernmost island created by Bathala,
our lovely Luzon, just north of the River Pasig."

My father whispered, "You mean . . . our own river?"
"Yes, and their children and grandchildren became
we Filipinos. You and I, my son, are

descended from that divine, royal line:
Aman Sinaya, Bathala, Malakas, Maganda,
the bamboo reed split open by Amihan."

As Nanay finished the tale, Martin, my Papa,
kissed her then went to play. My grandmother,
before she once again became Fructuosa

the Fish-Seller off to work at the market,
reveled in the thought that she herself
was the bamboo reed, the mother of mothers.

Such dreaming helped her through birth upon birth,
the death of her oldest daughter, a world war,
husband and son in the Bataan death march.

Fructuosa . . . shower of golden mangoes, windfall.
Rich brown called *kayumanggi,* she passed on to us.
Wife, mother, grandmother: life source, the well.

Maureen Tolman Flannery

Reeds

On the floating islands of Lake Titicaca
life, both sturdy and fragile,
is upheld by supple reeds
that grow in the marshy shallows
and give themselves like air
in and out of and around and under
the Uru people, who,
out of need and ingenuity,
fashioned these tatami carpets
thrown over floor of ice-blue water.

Better than having the best
is having the will
to make better use of what you have.
The sun-god Inti gave some men gold
in the soil and the core of old mountains.
To others, he gave these lake-shore reeds
for their rest and toil.
And all his people knew themselves
to be uniquely blessed. Long ago
didn't the wise ones take totora reeds
they found in the gentle whispers of the lake
to make straw-ground
for living on profound reaches of middle water.

What we might see as weeds became,
to right eyes, the foundations of life.
Pull them from thin rim-waters of the sacred lake
and begin to imagine what you might make
of the pithy, impervious husks.
Lash them into bundles you can curve, like ribs
into a boat to carry you to the shore.
Raise the walls of your home and its roof
against Andean rains.
Make every container that carries
what little you own or use.

Burn reed fuel to cook the reed's core
that will feed you.
Weave the earth that will support your weight;
weave your island, your plot, your home's floor.
Weave the place where your children will play.
Take reeds from where they shoot up in abundance
and make ground where you found none.

And is it not an illusion
that anyone stands on firmer earth than this?
Their lives atop these islands slowly drift
with the shift of time and misgivings.
Who's to say it's more precarious
than sure shore footing?
Ground-of-basket quietly answers back
the call of each footfall
as it gives but does not give way.
If you tread lightly on the insubstantial
the weight you levy on the ground lessens.
Perhaps the heart grows lighter
and the bones less dense
as the body learns
to sway gently in a lake breeze
like the barely-rooted reeds.

Madeline Artenberg

In the Land of the Snows

Bound by bamboo to shroud mist mount,
you haunch-sit hungry in your tree den
like a distraught Buddha.

Two blank eyes seize yours –
you sit up, neck strong
stare down, rocks shift –
a monk's ripped body rolls,
his eyes close.

You slump safe against a shrub
on a rug of damp skin,
hook with your forefoot pads
hollow two-foot shoots,
grown through the holes
in the monk's pierced chest.
You-chew-from-end-to-blood-fed-end,
eat-ing-bam-boo-eat-ing-bam-boo…

James A. McGrath

A Space for Light

On the reservation's edge
    they wait
    upright,
    brittle,
    as if they had been planted
    for harvesting.

Cattails, tules of all description,
    devil's-claw,
    willow,
    maidenhair fern,
    reeds for their kinship
    between weavers of baskets and the earth.

The hands ply silent strings of music
    into rings upon rings,
    the reeds forming birds, mountains, deer,
    images as ancient as finger prints.

These are the fragile reeds
    that grow out of the heart
    into fingers,
    into baskets that hold a space for light.

John Gilgun

Softstem Bulrush

Look,
how luminous
the reduplicate
softstem bulrushes,
above the silver-flashing alewives,
the single sunfish and the yellow perch.
As we float through them
they open for us, like doors
opening into rustling rooms,
making a sound like a broom
sweeping up breakfast crumbs
from a sun-struck kitchen floor.
Look, the infant Moses, floating
in his basket, a sedge-warbler
sitting beside him, reading to him
from a clay tablet, the legend of Ba and Ka.

Kristin Camitta Zimet

My Passover

I will not lean at ease to celebrate
the girl whose dry throat clamps
by the river of blood,
the boy whose muddy skin is shot with boils,
nor the red angel oozing under the nursery sill.
Not on this night or any other night.

I will not dance to the stallion's scream,
to the charioteer on his first campaign,
face down in salt.
I will not pour sweet wine to toast the lie,
the stubbornness of one man makes it just
to blight one thousand.

This night is different. Two strangers wade
into the Nile; between them reeds
rattle like spears.
One lets her newborn heart float out;
one catches to her breast
the child of the enemy, of another faith.

Katharyn Howd Machan

A Life

    for Tom Longin

A man may be a basket
woven with moon
and wave and fragile root,
all colors, few colors,
the sound of blue wind blowing
hard, silence of snow's

first breath. He may
offer a circle of sturdy
promise, place where hands
make real work matter,
sweet grain, an apple's curve.
A man may take his years

and wing a pattern of lake
and word and April sky
around the world he's chosen
to give, the strength of him
in others' good use, taking
shape that lasts and lasts.

Reeds to Salvation

My mother's brother, James Mangan,
always "Jake," never finished high school,
but became a General Man at the First
National Bank in Chicago, anyone off/out
and he stepped in, any function in the bank,
and then the real him would emerge at
night, remembering the jazz clubs, night
clubs in Chicago, the Alternative World,
Mr. Sax, "The secret's in the reeds, right
reed, right read, wrong reed, it all becomes
a blur....," dying at 86 out in the Nevada
desert, out playing under full moons, his
old Czech-Jew mother living with them,
"Who needs neighbors? Just me and the
coyotes....we know who we are."

Barbara Crooker

After September 11

If I say *God is good*,
you nod, because you also believe.
But if I say *My God is the one true God*,
that's when the troubles start. So many wars,
waged in the name of peace. *My missiles
are bigger than your missiles*. In the end,
when we are dust, will it matter who won?
One blue sky, fragile as a robin's egg,
covers us all. When we sleep, grass
is our last blanket. Maybe the stars
spell different stories to you, to me,
but in the darkness of the night,
they are light enough to see by.

Marianne Poloskey

Rifles and Roses

> For my husband Lou

With your bayonet
you used to cut a rose
to wear
in your rifle—
a rose
the color of a heart.

Instead of shooting,
you played
in an Army band.

As I write,
someone
in another country
on another continent
may be
listening to music—
without realizing
what he owes
to a clarinet.

Nancy Sather

How We Came to Music

Music was our first
language. We were conceived
to a beating drum,
our mother's heart, pounding
mere inches above our heads,
the surge of her blood
against the placental sponge.

We were weaned with the whistling of wind
through reeds, the flute song
of its voice, keening through cracks
between rocks and trees;
or the note breath made in the blowpipe
after the spear had flown.

Our fathers knew from the ring of the bow
how taut was the string. How it changed
with the tightening.
In its plucking we must have first known
the music of strings.

Charles Adés Fishman

A Field in Virginia

A wide gate swings open…
The hip-high grass children hid in
only two days ago has been mown.

Wade through the gold-leafed waves,
the rose-headed clover; walk
the shadowy edge of the field.

Over this river of cut grass
the sparrow hawk circles. The sun
blurs your footsteps in this world.

Walk out again when the sun
burns down the sky and the blue
sharpness of daylight is a white haze

on the hills. That fragrance you breathe
is the heart of the seed split open.
Press firmly on this green earth,

this sea of life you tread on.
Something will spring alive in you
and root down.

Kathleen S. Burgess

Gardening with Wallace Stevens

The mist was to light what red / Is to fire.
　　—Wallace Stevens
　　"Variations on a Summer Day"

I

Say that a black snake vanishes into bamboo
beyond the empty sleeve of its skin.

II

Naked, unselfconscious, the snake crosses
through tongues of zebra grass and silver grass
while the west wind plays grass harp—
a shushing, a mothering sound.

III

Grasses of the garden are fixed feathers
that lift and fluster, grown from worms
and peat and clay, to line their nests
with last year's desiccate stems.

IV

Over far hills the evening sun bears life
on round shoulders. It is always setting
through mimosa and maple, drifting cumulus,
mountain, sea, and forecasts of thunderflash,
rising cure and curse of the world that was, is.

V

Nature imagined through stained glass
says a snake is an omen of loss,
the loss, someone driven from grace,
the snake, danger of dangers, knowledge,
like a sun, the eye that never closes.

VI

Neighborhood boys see a snake. Not sure
of their duty. Should they rid my yard
of the beast to make the world safe?

VII

They can never make the world safe.
Then should they study it, poke it, leave it
alone? The best they can do is to let the snake
go the way of testing insect and rodent.

VIII

The snake grows as the adolescent grows,
muscular, drinking air.

IX

Raindrops prism leaf-edge rainbows, echo
celosias' flamboyant red, fire-brick orange,
lightning yellow, cactus brightening green.
Tradescantia begins to simmer deeper blue;
violet salvia to indigo. Like broken promises,
shadows slither.

X

On a fiery French marigold, a slug slimes
up from cedar mulch. The marigold, that repels
most insects, is to be a tracery, a lace
more delicious by tonight's star-stalked moon.

XI

Plant, slug, snake, and I are imprinted
from the egg, Alkumuna, from first light.

XII

In the shifting atmosphere of prisms, words
vein the body of the world we
know, we become, under a breaking sun.

Charlene Fix

Unmown Spaces

Acres of unmown grass waved like water.
In went the dog to his tail, the son
to his cap, the man to his waist,
the woman to her chest, and before them
grouse flew. The sea parted,
lapped them in grassy waves,
then closed again. They were Jews
passing through it, and Egyptians drowned
who didn't weep or flail: it was return.
Their hair bore seeds like stars,
and they drifted in the uncountable,
wandered in the undisturbed, which
swallowed them, wheatlike and leafy.

Douglas A. Fowler

chorus no. 1

    for Sonny Criss

reeds in marsh water
pierce the moon's reflection.

J.E. Robinson

Miriam

I put my brother in the water.

                      In a basket,

like Moses, and hoped Pharaoh's

daughter would draw him forth

                      to raise

as I did not want him.

The basket buffeted about

with his cries.

                      It went

against the bulrushes and sank

into the mud. Hours later,

                      Mom shrieked

an Earthless sound. My brother

was dead. Good riddance.

Jennifer Bosveld

Autopsy

i'll tell you now there is only poetry inside this body
and uncountable cuts yet i did not die from a workshop
slasher and no one killed me with feedback. i would
not change a word on his account with a gun to my
head and the father of poetry therapy says nobody ever
died from an overdose of poetry. i say read plath who
kept her dark spiral falling. i've tried to diversify but
find when i escape to the swap meet poetry is there and
at the dairy queen and movies. chelsea walls, wings of
desire, sweet hereafter. a book's worth if i care to
write it on the dull side of columbus. doesn't matter
what the paper says. poetry made me live and die it is
impartial in its murder impartial as disasters. i
would have signed a certificate it's what killed me but
my pen was radical, headed for trouble, and i as usual
was running after it.

Gina M. Tabasso

Pathétique

(Sonata in C Minor, Op. 13, by Ludwig van Beethoven)

You turn sheet music the way I turn
pages in a book. Our fingers have been known
to spark, to ivory, to paper, to pour over skin.
There you are next to your piano,
and I with my smooth ink.
We tell ours and others' stories, the tones
and discord of life. We touch in a way
most can't, and we learn that hands and fingers
are more valuable than legs or breasts—
the sex of the song, the crest of the poem.
You see notes on my body. I see words
on yours. And in this rampage, this grave
dance, this romp and repetition,
I can feel the pressure of the air
we hold in our lungs.

Leonard Orr

The Music We Play

In your note you said that when you
were lying across the seat, your head on my chest,
my left arm curved around your left shoulder,
caressing your long, fine neck and left arm,
my right hand stroking your stomach,
sometimes straying down towards your legs,
that you thought I was playing you
like a guitar, a metaphor that took root with me.

I would like to send soft breaths through you
like a small terra cotta ocarina held in my hands;
I would like to tap you and hear the sounds
you'd make, like a wooden Aztec tongue drum
(I'd happily drum my tongue, drum your tongue).
Like a hurdy-gurdy, I would sound your chanters
and spin your drones until your bridge buzzes.
I'd be like your bass recorder, and you would
play with traditional Baroque fingering;
I'd be your highland bagpipes, your own bombard,
your double-reed Turkish duduk, your Thai kaen;
your Japanese shakuhachi, your Andean panpipes.

It's wondrous, the process of playing together in harmony,
the way we resonate and complement each other.
My tongue in your ear tightens your ribcage
while you turn my tuning pegs with nimble fingers;
my testing thick thumb strums across your hips
while you tense my nipples with your lips,
plucking my chest hairs like a two-string dan tinh,
an Irish bouzouki, a moon-faced yuet chin.
Somehow we sound perfect together, though
you play me like a didgeridoo and we thump like dumbeks,
we squeeze each other like concertinas, and suddenly
we sound together like a rack of Javanese gongs.

Tony D'Arpino

Undated Valentine

    to Wendy

island shaped
like a lake
or a cave

outside
the dry reeds
move in the wind

objects
in moonlight
are possible

inside the ink
dries on pages
filled with tiny arrows

what we are willing
at any given skin
to offer chaos

Danny di Crispino

Drinking Scene on an Attic Vase

    vase painting by Oltos

she reclines in nakedness
enjoying the music

removing the double-aulos from her lip
just long enough to drink a glass of wine

only the arm of Dionysus can be seen
taking back the silver cup

standing out of vision
as she falls deeply back into music

the ivory instrument in her hands
the reedy sounds that intoxicate

wine and melody together reveal the skies
to a maenad or a bacchante

the women
frenzied by either that touch their lips

she immerses herself in
the music of the spheres

the unheard sounds
only a raving woman could hear

or appreciate

Nancy Wall

Syrinx

She'd eluded so many, this daughter of Diana,
that when Pan started after her one night
she must have thought she could outrun him.
But ugliness had made him desperate, swift.
And fleeing the click of hooves on rock
tumbling behind her down the mountainside,
she lost her confidence. She reached the river
just ahead of him and tried to hide herself
among the reeds. Dreading the touch
of the hairy, horned seducer, reeking
of old goat skins, she begged protection
from her sister nymphs.

You can't blame them for what followed—
their intention was pure, they had
no time to consider consequences.
Surely he wouldn't find her there, just another
reed among the others? How could they know
he'd pluck a whole armload? If he couldn't
possess her as nymph, he would have her
anyway, imprisoned in a pipe.

So Pan continues his pursuits, and Syrinx,
sentenced in that transforming moment
to eternal regret, must wish she'd sacrificed
herself in one unspeakable act that would
at least have ended. Enduring forever his foul,
hot breath is suffering enough—but she
must also bear the knowledge that her sweet,
unwilling tone joins others to lend power
to his seductions. And like her sister nymphs
she carries guilt for what she cannot change.

Pan thinks he silenced her, consumed her
voice in his. But sometimes when he sleeps
and the wind sweeps in from the right direction,
one clear, high note rises above his snores
to sing her story, a dirge that slides down centuries.

Danny di Crispino

Sharette dedicates a song to her daughter, conceived by a rape, and to her son-in-law on their wedding day.

Sharette was playing Debussy's *Syrinx*
on her flute
when a sparrow flew into the church.

She stood unaware,
stiff in the music,
her face almost prosthetic,
embouchure uneven as she played.

People laughed
at the bird crashing red
into the stained glass windows,

intoxicated, perhaps, by music,
like Pan by the nymph turned to reeds.

      *

When Sharette came out of her coma
twenty-two years before,
she had hysterical blindness,
only able to see light, nothing more.

His face, everything else,
forced from her memory.

The doctors puzzled together
the shattered bones with metal and plastic,
transforming nose, cheek, mouth,
filling what cracks they could
to save one eye.

She wouldn't have recognized
her face in a mirror
when her vision returned.

When at last she saw her flute
she didn't remember that she played,
but her fingers found their way to the keys.

She learned the haunting music by ear,
and for the first time played for her daughter,
groom, congregation,
and the unseen, lost bird.

      *

Slashed, stitched, transformed.
she is a vessel of music, like Syrinx,
skin cut and bound into unequal lengths,
the air spun inside pouring out.

She couldn't stop gazing at her daughter
until the final diminuendo—nymph's last call.
Church silenced. Bird,
rising.

Kristin Berkey-Abbott

Damnable Instruments

I have piped miracles
with this flute. Even when the Nazis
shut us out of their culture, we created
our own operas and orchestras.
They took away our instruments, but I could hide
my flute. And we could always sing.

My flute bought my passage out. I hated to sell
it, but a trade for a ticket to freedom
seemed fair. And I got a job teaching tiny
fingers to work magic on shrunken pipes.

Then the letters streamed in. Every family
member left behind implored me to find
a way to rescue them. I did my best,
but I was no Pied Piper. Besides, Hitler's
ears, deaf to the magic of music, certainly would pay
no attention to my desperate notes.
And music teachers made such little bits of money.

My mother's correspondence grew increasingly desperate.
She accused me of hardening my heart,
of only being interested in my music,
the way I'd always been. Did she not know
of my frantic attempts which consumed
all my free time while my new flute pouted
in its case? Did she not meet me
in my nightmares, not see me watching
in the shadows, unable to stop her tortures?

Damnable instrument. Every time I touch
it, I think of my mother's hysterical accusations
that I love my flute more than her. I cease
all playing, cut my teaching ties.
I get a job selling shoes and sturdy
boots, so much more practical than
ethereal music.

James Reiss

Schilfgraben

is German for "reedy ditch." I read it yesterday
on a plaque under a painting of marshland.
When I reached the top of the spiral-tiered gallery,
I stared six stories down at a fountain jetting
and thought of particulars, the proper
names for ferns and vine-hungry moths.

I make a wish for Clara whose hair was straw-yellow.
In my journal one summer I called her "my willowy reed."
I wrote: "Clara's waist-long hair made me feel
like Rilke beside her today as we hiked down a slope
toward the Danube over swampy areas
locally known as The Sedge."

Not one straw-yellow strand lasts, saved
between the pages of my journal, to tell me
she is more than the hollow stalk of a phrase.
Yet I wrote: "She wore a barrette
and braided the dough she baked
in ovens that made me think of Treblinka."

I think of half-tracks, tanks,
the dominance of one idea
without regard for particulars.
Then I imagine Clara hatless in 1980,
leaning over a rolling pin or pounding
dough with her fists.

Shy as a marsh bird, mired behind a counter,
she bags pumpernickel, rye,
says *Auf Wiedersehen* to a customer,
and scribbles on a pad: "These tablespoons,
these numbered measuring cups,
dole out the bread of life."

Sara Littlecrow-Russell

Her Baskets

The elders used to say that baskets,
if they are well made, will give life to seeds.
Her baskets are like that,
Manidoowaadizi—something inherent spiritual,
woven with precision
from reeds, ash splints, sweetgrass,
and woman spirit
made to hold with a perfect fit
her dreams of a traditional Indian man.

She weaves until she has
a table full of empty baskets
and she fills them with paper dolls
(so Indian on the outside)
and seed chaff (so empty in between)
they're just for now she says….
and she goes on filling her baskets
with what she's got
and the baskets go on trying
to breathe life into seed husks
when the kernel is gone.

Sarah Brown Weitzman

Yellow Corn Woman's Third Daughter

Yellow Corn Woman's third daughter has said
I may come to her tonight in the place

called Where Dawn Strikes Late.
I will leave the village when the moon rests

above the southern pines to be there before her
to spread the grass with small chips of cedar.

Twice today Yellow Corn Woman's third daughter
has rubbed herself clean with cold creek water.

All day she has chewed fragrant leaves
of the bay tree. Tonight she will bring a basket

of warm corn and bear fat cakes, two green fruits
and a softened root. Four black shaman's snakes

will twine in pairs as the moonlight ripples
over her braided hair and the night wind will whisper

her name—Slender Reed. And afterwards, we will chant
our fathers' prayers for many, oh, many strong, straight sons.

Sheryl L. Nelms

Rowing Across Wild Rice Lake

you are wind
I am reeds

make me bend
and writhe

James A. McGrath

Sky of Reeds

The roof is woven thatch,
    three feet of river reeds.

On the underside of the roof,
    just above the crossbeams,
    the reeds are blackened by decades
    of wood smoke.
    Thin webs of soot wave
    in the updrafts of heat
    from our hibachi.

Our roof is a place of mysterious voices,
    sounds of spring birds, summer insects,
    winter mice, night bats.

Our roof has reeds extinct now.
    The river gone, paved over,
    only a pocket of dampness
    on the hillside.

My ancestors live in our sky of reeds.
    One day I shall join them and
    the song of the river.

Lynn Veach Sadler

A Disquisition upon Thatch on the Way to Jane Austen's

On the way to Jane Austen's home
in Chawton Village, Alton, Hampshire,
our guide forewarns us to watch for thatch.
Thatch is precious to the English—
and to their tourists.
One has one's thatching done
by Master Thatcher or Country Gentleman.
Guide and husband chose the former,
who recommended reed rather than straw;
though more expensive,
reed is quite the "toney" thing.
So, reed thatch it was (and is).

In Chawton Village, Alton, Hampshire, too,
are many, many thatched reed roofs.
But not just plain—oh, no!—
they are replete with
the thatcher's signature:
two thatched pheasants
grace the roof line.
"Oh, pheasants under grass," I say aside,
though knowing our guide would relegate grass
to the disgrace of straw.
On the far side of the roof,
when I look back,
a china cat—or is it perhaps plain pottery?—
stalks the superior pheasants
in their pheasantry.
But I digress.

When I turn back, our guide is saying thatch
is the source of hats-worn-in-the-house and
canopied four-posters.
"Nesting creatures dropped, you see,
from the thatch upon their heads."

I have no time to ponder
these thatched heads,
for I must concentrate upon
the excess costs of insurance for the thatched,
though gutters aren't required with thatch,
and thatch absorbs water.
"Because the bedroom was upstairs
and had no ceiling,
only thatch, the bed must have protection.
Though now the thatch is bound
with mesh of wire,
the wire's no guarantee.
Small creatures still get in."
"What a creature comfort," I say aside.
Then I digressed again:

"What about Jane Austen's house?"
"Oh," she said, "it is not thatched
and never has been."

Sharon Scholl

Electronic Clarinet: A Lament

No hint of creek banks
from the sensuous tremble
of shaped reed floating
down the tongue's pink muscle.
Nothing of the lungs' veined
transparent filament
expiring in a slender shaft
of air made audible.
Tone without systolic punctuation
or metabolic pulse,
betraying no mortal frailty
of lip or fingers.
Unbearable perfection
of pitch and tempo, a musical
machine gun with an endless
tonal ammo clip.
Born sterile on a bed
of calculus and circuit
diagrams, fathered by a feed-
back loop for brainless
rote persistence.
Here in the celestial silence
of the Sunday offertory
we startle at its strange
metallic sneering
of Bach's "Air in D."

Daniel M. Gallik

Linn Seeks the Musings of Music

Her new beau she met at Severance,
near the Art Museum she went to
to find a rich guy. Liam said to
her as he was tightening his reeds,

I like to speak of recuperating
my oboe, like I am nursing it,
kind of accelerating it back to
good health because for like ten

years it existed in the closet.
Linn looked into his eyes, they
were around sixty-five years old,
and said, I love a man who knows

wind. He said, you are quite
rich in your interpretations. May
I ask your moniker? Linn said,
Linn. And Liam said, I am, yes,

this Liam McGonagle, originally
of Northern Ireland, straight
west of Scotland. I shall never
say England. Linn said, I do,

yes, like your music, and hope
that it makes love well, that it
touches my singing love triangle
in a most delicate way on stage.

Sherman Pearl

Woodwinds

I give you this clarinet, child. It's ten thousand years old,
conceived by the first musician, the genius who

blew on his hands to warm them and heard music
pour out. It's the descendent of goat horns and bladders;

hornpipes and hollowed-out reeds still echo in the wood.
When you play it, the breath of ancients

who called to their gods through clay pipes and conch shells
will blow behind yours. The mouthpiece is marked

by all the serfs who played jigs on whistles to ward off
the plague, by all the herdsmen who tootled

their hearts out in lonely pastures, by every piccolo player
whose pips have drowned in the orchestra's din.

Their lips will press down on yours; the bite
will cut into yours till you know the pain in the music.

Your fingers will be guided by all the jazzmen who've
perched on tenement sills wailing their stories

in 2/4 time, reaching for notes that only angels can find,
releasing them into the night like messenger birds.

Child, I give you the tired old tunes I've finished playing.
You'll squeak them a while; and when the tone grows

clear as the song in your head you'll improvise.
You'll noodle, you'll reach, you'll add one note to the score.

Kenneth Salzmann

Paul Desmond's Last Date at Symphony Hall, Boston

So many have walked this wall
in just this way that their footfalls, too,
are beaten in sambas and rondos
into the hidden tempos of the street;
yours come down at stage door
in five-four paces,
encircling ghostly wisps of breath,
gathering again in a new confusion
of entrances and exits reedy melodies
drawn from a muscle-memory of riffs
that how often have skitted
through those horns
in cool approximations of redemption.

George Held

Phragmites' Foe

    For Jean

Even the labors of Hercules
Included no task so epic
As defeating mighty Phragmites
On the banks of Long Pond.

Hacking and sawing away, you spent
The Season bent over in knee-deep muck,
Obscure within the Greenbelt's woods
While others swam and sunned at the beach.

Why did you assume this thankless task,
Playing Mrs. Sisyphus,
The odds of extirpating this thick reed
No better than rolling that big stone

Up to the top of the hill without
The sickening thrill of seeing it
Tumble back down again and again,
Just as Phragmites will send shoots

Up from its watery base each spring?
Still, your work gave other, native, plants
A chance to reassert themselves
In the space you cleared on the bank.

For this your satisfaction came
From keeping your covenant
With Nature, to help keep invasives out
And let natives keep their tenuous grasp.

Jen Karetnick

What Goes in by the Hand Goes out by the Hand

I loved a boy who played music
on his hands, rippled whole octaves
through his thumbs, compressed

his palms for pitch. Even air
can be held, and surprise;
he walked around days breathing

skies into birds and empty
churches into oceans. Though his mother
typed "clarinet" on his music camp

application, he never quite grasped
its hawking reed, keys constantly
escaping, so unlike the hands

he arched to his lips by instinct
to fill space with more pulsing space.

Vanessa Kittle

Driftwood

Dol goes out in his green canoe.
He carefully pushes it from the bank,
slides it through the brackish water,
swallows the bottle of pills.

He paddles slowly from his wicker seat
admiring the geese, the ducks, the gulls,
and of course, his reeds:
the ones he gathered for his grandmother
when his boat was still large enough
to brave the swells of blue oceans.

There are places on the river
where he cannot see any signs of man,
but then there is the bulldozer.
In the past he would have clenched his jaw at this,
but not today. Today he simply paddles.

He lies back to admire the clouds.
They make him smile
and keep his eyes wide.

A clamdigger finds him first,
sees the staring face,
then quickly motors on.
It would be dangerous to get involved.

The tide floats the little green canoe
out to the bay to Miranda,
who is wading up to her hips.
She peers over the side,
considers taking him in,
but something about his expression changes her.
She gives him a gentle push instead,
and out he goes—
eyes wide—
listening to the waves and the birds
and staring at the clouds.

Elizabeth Ann James

Bamboo

1967. Bass Lake. The summer house the island.
Mom wears an amethyst bracelet
& three garnet rings when she plays "Deep Purple."
My sister Christine
hunts a ping-pong ball
finds the Edison Talking Machine in a closet
the dog on its haunches the trumpet flower
everything we crave to wind
yet there is no needle.
Fondling discs as heavy as dinner plates
& using a magnifying glass we read:
Art Tatum's "Black Swamp Rag—Hold That Tiger"
Adelina Patti's "Last Summer Rose."
"No needle?" Unc says, "I'll make one
you'll hear Caruso the best needles
are bamboo" & with a flash
of his pen knife he
cuts a splice from a fish pole
his thick agile fingers
rapidly insert the splinter into
the heavy bent arm of the Victrola
I hear it now *Celeste Aida ah ah my
divina* the notes cold & pure
run with the Au Sable.

Richard Terrill

Five Reasons Not to Play the Tenor Saxophone

Its shape curved like grace turned back
on itself is like lost love

Its green brass lake and oil smell
remains all night on your hands

The cold mouthpiece you must blow
into with an o of the
lips as one blows into a
fist on a cold afternoon
often produces music
you hadn't thought of before

The reed you must hold up to
light to see its cane heart—if
you put it in your mouth and
try to talk no one will know
what you are trying to say

The flowers etched in lacquer
on the gold bell

Matthew Thorburn

To an Oboe

If we can agree "there's a music for everybody,"
      as Eric Salzman says, then yours
is mine. Double reed, narrow bell, dark shine

      of grenadilla wood from the Mpinga tree,
I'd never confuse you with a clarinet.
      Your "penetrating, brilliant tone"—I might

say *arch*, a touch *reedy*, though not so high
      as a *whine*—seems at home with a violin, viola
and cello in this Quartet in F Major

      by Mozart, though in my *Webster's* you elbow in
comfortably enough between *obnubilate*,
      "to be cloudy, becloud," and *obol*, "the ancient

Greek coin or weight equal to 1/6 drachma,"
      even if in the illustrative sketch you appear
to be played by Steve Martin. Still I hear you

      best in the *Peter and the Wolf* I heard a dozen
years ago at St. Gerard's, in which you're the duck
      who waddles, quacks and too quickly

gets gulped down for lunch by the bandy-legged
      wolf skulking about in velvet breeches,
but not quite, not yet, not before

      you paddle past once more in the cool dark
waters that flow from B flat below
      middle C upwards for over 2½ octaves.

Donna Pucciani

Hautbois and the Night Visitors

The oboists in the pit are sucking cane. The Magi,
shattering the footlights with rubies and topaz,
have already marched to the hut of the impoverished
widow with the crippled son. Amahl, not yet cured,
flings himself on his crutch towards the star
projected onto the cobalt-curtained sky.

Twin oboes, side by side, compulsively
lip their reeds with redeeming spit,
just enough to render the double reeds pliable,
friendly. No arguments tonight. The peasants bring
olives and quinces, mignonettes and camomile
to the Kings seeking the child
who belongs to the poor.

The drumbeats have started, steady, irrefutable.
Fear gurgles, but never mind. Emerging from their world
of shot glasses, saliva, and slivers of wood,
the oboists test the tenderness of their song
on high serpentine notes, slipping into them like cobras,
licking the dance that sounds more like a belly-dancer
than a shepherdess in rags waving tambourines and figs.

First one oboe, then the other,
rolls in the tangled sweat of rosewood ecstasy
until the orchestra enters and they can breathe.
Silent, relieved, they know the real miracle will happen
only long after they have finished their twisted
little tunes, and the shepherds have put to bed
their babies and sheep. The curtain will close
when the hungry are sated, the children made whole.
Imagine from the dark cave under the stage
the light of the laser-beamed star.

Paula Chertok

In Memory

He taught me that music is not the notes,

but what happens between the notes—

a link, a sculpting of sound,

a breath that slants the flame but does not blow it out.

> Dedicated to Marc Lifschey, late principal oboe,
> Cleveland Orchestra and San Francisco Symphony

Marta Ferguson

Sax

(Breathe)
Lingering blind over the first crescendoed riff
you slide your fingers down over the keys
as you coax the saxophone to sing for me
alone in the practice room
(Breathe)
The pulsing sounds that you command
waver smoothly into throbbing vibrato
I echo the music, body tensed
eyes closed, lips apart, thought suspended
(Breathe)
Flying, eyes half-open, through the decrescendoed fall
you ease your fingers off the keys,
putting the saxophone aside for me
alone in the practice room
   (   )

Robert Samarotto

Body and Soul

The new kid on the block
plays a tenor saxophone
impossibly—like an outlaw.
He curls his lips
around the mouthpiece.
His tongue darts and flutters
against the reed.
Hefty-throated,
honey-colored sounds
stain the air:
camphor blues,
languid ambers,
sighing, drooping yellows,
raging purples,
sliding greens,
growling sepias.

He slouches and sways
with the sweet-talking brass
that glows under lissom hands.
He moans and bellows
with closed eyes,
a wide vibrato—
"Body and Soul."

The rapping on his door
is not from a secret admirer.
The piano police have tracked him down
and before his song is finished
will arrest him
for indecent use of the imagination.

Steve Abbott

Arresting Saxophones

    for Charlie Parker

Stalin hummed an old folk song
as he stood at the window the way he stood,
in heavy boots, on everything.
He knew what he was doing when he outlawed
the saxophone, had every glittering horn arrested
without first-hand knowledge of its power
in women's eyes, their red dresses and lips.
Men, too, betrayed within the sound,
how it weaves itself around desire or pain
and pushes to the surface like a piece of
metal buried in flesh, long after the war
wounds have healed and only now and then
squawk like a bent note in the solo.

As if lifted by wings each pulse quickens,
becomes a broad brush or fine-line dauber
to record entire palettes of midnight, mixing
a weary wisdom with each piece of sadness
drawn bubbling into something bigger
than its own stagnant pool, where mosquitoes
dance tiny needles, prance like handkerchiefs
in a second line or white horses in a military funeral.
Nothing else can raise eyes like this,
no political hero or medaled marshal
has this voice, this thin and powerful wind
over a wild reed vibrating green in the shallows
of that cool lake at the bottom of the soul,
closed eyes seeing the ripples moving inward.
The vibrations catch this light, illuminate
everything worth knowing about
proletarian democracy, heads nodding in unison
or swaying side to side in counterpoint
as each player makes his own arrangement
of the familiar, the changes a future to build on.

The patterns measured by hands on tables
are not marching feet, no matter the rhythm.

The clear notes, raw, smooth, murmured or shouted
hang in the air above the packed house
on wings wider than eleven time zones,
above high-hat's whispered shiver a liquid
tumble of sounds on a spiraling updraft rush,
feathered breath stealing every loyalty to lover or god
and leaving a rich hush in every lung,
ready to explode whoops and shouts
when the kick drum, snare, piano pick him up and
drop the crowd back into the melody as the big arm of
the bass wraps around the room's shoulders and
starts strutting with a trumpet pushed forward,
dancing in creased pants for a few measures
through the changes that keep the blues coming,
keep people coming back for more
of his hummingbird hovering and diving,
awash in a cascade of notes from the stage,
where his black forehead is a blaze of white water.
Bird's drinking it in—the room, the light,
early morning already reaching the horizon,
where an army is gathering to improvise
its own sense of order.
The rifles rattle arhythmic notes.
Each soldier unconsciously taps a foot.

Richard Terrill

Flight

At Wal-Mart in my town, in a bin
with Mantovani and Mitch Miller,
Charlie Parker blows another chorus of "Crazeology."
The tape's so cheap it kinks up
in my box when I get it home,
the auto-reverse kicks in in the middle of Bird's ride,
and suddenly the out chorus of "Quasimodo" blares tinny
through my bookshelf speakers, the "b" side. And then another wrinkle
and we're back to Parker's solo again, the same licks
we just heard. It's said

Bird never repeated an idea.

There was a time in my life I didn't like bebop.
There was something wrong with me. I thought
music should move slowly enough that I could hear,
this before days like today
when I came home from work
and blew hard bop licks during the noon hour
on my tenor sax in the basement.
Before I liked bebop I thought most phenomena
could be explained.

The tape's cover art is an old black
and white photo, Bird's slouched frame cut out and tinted
in primary colors. His eyes
bulge as if caught in a lie, his shirt hot pink
and tie mottled blue.

There are no liner notes. Who are the other players?
Diz? Max Roach? My Aunt Mildred? Who
on the live tracks
like "Marmaduke" or "Groovin' High,"
which burn like lit fire,
who are all those people talking
in the background?

Why aren't they listening, in this unnamed club
to this unspecified rhythm section
in this world never quite identified enough?
The gray sheet of their conversation thrown over the art
is like a second drummer
with a sizzle cymbal and a tendency
to rush a little.
I can hear glasses clank, voices compete
for attention.
Somebody's trying to pick somebody up
back there in 1948,
and I can almost hear his car pull away on 52nd Street
in the rain. I hope he got lucky. And the guy

who just came in—double-breasted seersucker suit,
the kind I would have worn—
who can't get the bartender's attention, who's mad the band's on break,
who just ended an argument with his wife
the way they always end
when somebody stops talking,
and so he stopped for smokes, came in the back,
passed a bloated black man lighting up a joint in the alley,
holding a soft-sided suitcase the size of an alto saxophone,
and going on about Stravinsky,
Bartok, and Henry Wallace. "Who in the hell,"
the angry husband asks, "is that Negro?"

David Williams

Listening to Coltrane's Blues

I want to climb
like the morning glory vine
of Coltrane's
soprano sax,

crazy tendrils
trying to teach
a chain-link fence
some tenderness,

open throat rasping
past limits, the golden
weight swung toward
the light.

Patricia Smith

Map Rappin'

    for John Coltrane, and forever for Bruce

I always shudder when I pray.

Mama say the Lord enters you in stages,
first like a match lit under your skin,
then like an animal biting through bone
with soft teeth. Mama say lie still
and wait for glory to consume you,
wrap its way into your map
like a lover had his finger on paradise,
knew the way with all his heart, then lost it.
I always shudder when I pray,
so your name must be a prayer.
Saying your name colors my mouth,
frees loose this river, changes my skin,
turns my spine to string. I pray all the time now.
Amen.

Try not to touch me while I tell this.
Try not to brush the thick tips of your fingers
against my throat while my throat moves
telling this story. Don't suddenly squeeze
my bare shoulder or travel your mouth
along the flat swell of my belly.
Don't bite at the hollow in my back,
whisper touch my ankles,
or match our skin like spoons.

Don't punctuate this rambling sentence
with your tongue or trace your name
on the backs of my legs,
please don't walk the question
of your breath along my thighs
or draw a map on my quivering breastbone
guiding me to you,

me to you,
me to you,
don't play me
that way

don't play me

that way

the way the saxman plays his woman,
blowing into her mouth till she cries,
allowing her no breath of her own.
Don't play me that way, baby, the way
the saxman plays his lady,
that strangling, soft murder—notes like bullets,
riffs like knives and the downbeat slapping
into her. and she sighs.
into her. and she cries.
into her.
and she whines like the night turning.

Let me sit here on the bar stool sipping something bitter.
Let me cross my legs,
slow
like the colored girls do,
and let me feel your eyes go there.
Let me feed on glory and grow fat.

Meanwhile, lover, let's fill this wicked church with music.
Let me lean into this story, for once,
without your mouth on me. The music a lit match
under my skin and I dance,
all legs and thunderous and heels too high,
I dance cheap perfume and black nail polish.
Sharkskin congregation, heads *pressed*,
attitudes too tight, won't scream

until it gets to be too much, won't beg for mercy
until I wreck the landscape with my hips.
Bar stools filling, everybody waiting for the glory
to move through me, fill me with hosannas,
rock me with hallelujahs, to shake these bored bones.
They wait for you, supreme love, to pull me out
onto the dance floor, make me kick my heels above my head.
High heels 'bove my nappy head.

While they wait, I will dance with the saxman,
I will shimmer as he presses my keys.
Him and me boppin', we are *wicked* church.
So don't play, do not play, did you hear me tell you
not to play me that way?
(The way I pray to be played.)

Mama say the Lord enters you in stages
(Play me that way)
First like a lit match under your skin
(Play me that way)
Then like an animal biting through bone with soft teeth
(Play me)
Mama say lie still and wait for glory
(that way)
to consume me
(that way)
Press my keys
(that way)
Press my keys
(that way)

Don't pay me no mind, lover.
I always shudder

when I pray.

Contributor Notes

Steve Abbott, "Arresting Saxophones," pp. 96-97, author of two chapbooks including a *Greatest Hits* collection (Pudding House, 2006), has work published in *The Connecticut Review*, *Big Scream*, *Slip Stream*, and *Evening Street Review*. An associate editor with Pudding House Publications, he recently edited the anthology *Cap City Poets*. He teaches at Columbus State Community College.

Madeline Artenberg, "In the Land of the Snows," p. 51. Her poetry appears in publications such as *Margie*, *The American Journal of Poetry*, *Vernacular*, and *The Absinthe Literary Review*. She has received several awards, including semi-finalist in the 2005 contest of *Margie*. Rogue Scholars published her poetry book *Awakened*.

Dick Bakken, "Old Bamboo Fishing Pole," p. 22, wrote this poem when he lived in Seattle. Since 1980 he has lived on the Mexican border in Bisbee, Arizona. His latest book is *Dick Bakken: Greatest Hits 1967-2002* (Pudding House Publications).

Caroline G. Banks, "Gazing Out Over Lotus," p. 43, received an honorable mention in The Society for Humanistic Anthropology's poetry contest. Her poetry appears in *Anthropology and Humanism Quarterly*, among other journals.

Roy Bentley, "Because If Things Are Not Carefully Hidden," p. 14, "Let It Grow" p. 23. His first book of poems was *Boy in a Boat*; his second, *Any One Man*. *The Trouble with a Short Horse in Montana* won the White Pine Poetry Prize and was published in 2006. He makes his home in Stuart, Florida. His web address is www.roy-bentley.com.

Kristin Berkey-Abbott, "Damnable Instruments," p. 74, has written in many different genres. Pudding House Publications published her chapbook *Whistling Past the Graveyard* in 2004. She teaches at the Art Institute of Fort Lauderdale and serves as Assistant Chair of General Education.

Jennifer Bosveld, "Autopsy," p. 66, has authored 18 books and chapbooks, conceptualized *virtual journalism* poetry (*Jazz Kills the Paperboy*), published textbook anthologies *Elastic Ekphrastic* and *Topics for Getting in Touch: the Applied Writing Sourcebook*. Jen innovated the *POETS GREATEST HITS* ™ national archive. Her Pudding House Publications boasts over 1500 titles in print.

Kathleen S. Burgess, "Poem for Patricia, and Ulli, and Ted," p. 16, and "Gardening with Wallace Stevens," pp. 61-62, is a *Confluence* Poetry Contest winner, Pushcart Prize nominee, and senior editor at Pudding House Publications. A chapbook *Shaping What Was Left* was published in 2006. Her poems appear in *North American Review*, *Sou'wester*, *Pavement Saw*, *Borderlands—the Texas Poetry Review*, *Evening Street Review*, and several anthologies.

Paula Chertok, "In Memory," p. 94. Her poetry has been published in various literary journals, including *The Gettysburg Review*. "In Memory" is dedicated to her late husband, oboist Marc Lifschey.

David Citino, "Neanderthal, with Help from Cave and Bear, Invents the Flute," p. 9, Poet Laureate of The Ohio State University, wrote over fourteen books including *The News and Other Poems* (University of Notre Dame Press), *A History of Hands*, (posthumous, The Ohio State University Press), and prose collection, *Paperwork* (Kent State University Press).

Allan Douglass Coleman, "La Opera," p. 15, Pushcart Prize nominee, writes poetry, fiction, and creative non-fiction, and produces various forms of visual art. He has published in *Cape Rock*, *Hazmat Review*, *International Poetry Review*, *Lalitamba*, *Nimrod*, *Pacific Review*, and elsewhere. He's online at villaflorentine.us.

Barbara Crooker, "After September 11," p. 57. Barbara Crooker won the Word Press First Book award for her full-length collection, *Radiance,* and her second book, *Line Dance* is also out from Word. New work is out in *Tampa Review*, *Poetry International*, *The MacGuffin, JAMA, Calyx*, and others.

Tony D'Arpino, "Undated Valentine," p. 69. His books include *Greatest Hits 1969-2003* (Pudding House Publications, 2004), *Seven Dials* (Kealakekua, 1997), *The Shape of the Stone* (Deep Forest, 1990). His poetry appears in *Bloomsbury Review*, *Pavement Saw*, *Poetry East*, *Runes,* and several anthologies.

Allison A. deFreese, "Barcelona," p. 28, is published in *Southern Poetry Review* and other journals as well as in the anthology *Rough Places Plain: Poems of the Mountains* (Salt Marsh Pottery Press, 2005).

Danny di Crispino, "Drinking Scene on an Attic Vase," p. 69, "Sharette dedicates a song to her daughter, conceived by a rape, and to her son-in-law on their wedding day." pp. 72-73. The 2007-2008 editor-in-chief of *Oyez Review*, he is currently completing his MFA in Creative Writing at Roosevelt University. His poetry has appeared in journals such as *Poems & Plays, Gargoyle,* and *Rambler*.

Marta Ferguson, "Sax" p. 93. A former poetry editor of *The Missouri Review*, she is sole proprietor of Wordhound Writing & Editing Services, LLC. Her poems appear or are forthcoming in *5am, Passages North, Prairie Schooner, Rattle, The Southeast Review, Iodine,* and *Poetry Daily.*

Charles Adés Fishman, "A Field in Virginia," p. 60. His most recent book-length collection, *Chopin's Piano*, received the 2007 Paterson Award for Literary Excellence. The revised second edition of his anthology, *Blood to Remember: American Poets on the Holocaust*, was published by Time Being Books in 2007.

Charlene Fix, "Unmown Spaces," p. 63, received a Robert H. Winner Memorial Award and several fellowships, has poems in *Chicago Review, The Journal, Rattle, Poetry*, collections *Flowering Bruno: A Dography* (XOXOX Press) and *Mischief* (Pudding House Publications), and teaches at Columbus College of Art & Design.

Maureen Tolman Flannery, "Reeds," pp. 49-50, a native of Wyoming, now lives in Chicago. Her latest books are *Ancestors in the Landscape* and *A Fine Line*. Her work has appeared in fifty anthologies and two hundred literary reviews, including *Calyx, Atlanta Review,* and *North American Review*.

Douglas A. Fowler, "chorus no. 1" p. 64, teaches physics at Youngstown State University. His first collection of poems, *Condensed Matter and Other States of Mind,* was published by Finishing Line Press in 2005. He says saxophonist Sonny Criss should be better remembered.

Hugh Fox, "Reeds to Salvation," p. 56, was born in Chicago in 1932. Of 110 books published, his most recent, *The Collected Poetry of Hugh Fox* (540 pages), was published by World Audience in NYC, 2008. He has 20 unpublished novels on shelves.

Allison Funk, "August's Prairie," p. 19. Allison Funk is the author of three books of poems: *The Knot Garden, Living at the Epicenter,* and *Forms of Conversion*. She teaches creative writing at Southern Illinois University Edwardsville.

Daniel M. Gallik, "Linn Seeks the Musings of Music," p. 83, disabled by a cerebral aneurysm, continues publishing with *Hawaii Review, A.I.M., Parabola, Nimrod, Hiram Poetry Review,* and *Whiskey Island*. Larger works include novels—*A Story Of Dumb Fate* (publishamerica.com), *Must Know Death* (available for publication)—and *Linn's Poems* (deepcleveland.com).

John Gilgun, "Softstem Bulrush," p. 53, has authored seven books, *The Dooley Poems* (Robin Price, 1991), *In the Zone: The Moby Dick Poems of John Gilgun* (Pecan Grove Press, 2002), *The Dailies: Poems by John Gilgun* (forthcoming, VRZHU Press), and hundreds of stories, poems, and essays.

Vince Gotera, "Born from Bamboo," pp. 46-48, is editor of the *North American Review* and an English professor at the University of Northern Iowa. His poetry collections include *Dragonfly* and *Fighting Kite* (Pecan Grove Press, 1994 and 2007), and *Ghost Wars* (Final Thursday Press, 2003).

George Held, "Phragmites' Foe," p. 86, has published thirteen collections of poems. His work has appeared in such places as Garrison Keillor's *Writer's Almanac, Confrontation, Connecticut Review,* and *Notre Dame Review,* and has been included in over a dozen anthologies.

Dory L. Hudspeth, "Café Foreplay," p. 24, of Alvaton, KY, is an herbalist, historical researcher, freelance writer, and poet. Word Tech Press published her first book, *Enduring Wonders*. A chapbook, *I'll Fly Away*, is available from Finishing Line Press.

Elizabeth Ann James, "Bamboo," p. 89, widely published, has won prizes including those sponsored by the James Joyce Journal of International Studies and The National League of American Pen Women. She writes about art for *The Short North Gazette*, and convenes *The Muses* and *Areopagitica Prose*.

Jen Karetnick, "What Goes in by the Hand Goes out by the Hand," p. 87, is author of chapbooks *Necessary Salt* (Pudding House Publications), *Bud Break at Mango House*, which won the 2008 Portlandia Prize, and *Eve and After*, which was a finalist in the Women of Words contest from Southern Hum Press.

Alexander Levering Kern, "Street Craft," p. 27. Poet, educator, and Quaker, his work appears in *Georgetown Review*, *Caribbean Writer*, *Rive Gauche*, and anthologies from St. Anthony Messenger Press, Ibbetson Street, among other publications. He is editor of *Becoming Fire: Spiritual Writing from Rising Generations*.

Vanessa Kittle, "Driftwood," p. 88, former chef, lawyer, now editor of *Abramelin*, www.abramelin.net, teaches English composition. She has three collections: a chapbook, *Apart*, and books *Surviving the Days of the Empire* (both The March Street Press, 2006) and *The Chatter of Birds* (Luciole Press, 2008).

Steve Lautermilch, "Grass Script, Kitty Hawk," p. 34, "The Wetlands Song" p. 35, poet and fine art photographer, has a new chapbook, *Fire Seed & Rain* (Longleaf Press). Solo exhibits were held in 2006 at the Festival Park Gallery, Manteo, North Carolina, and the Getchell Library Gallery of the University of Nevada, Reno.

Carol Lem, "Kyorei (Empty Bell)," p. 25, "Kurokami (Black Hair)" pp. 44-45. Her poems appear in *Chrysalis*, *Tebot Bach*, and *Red Rock Review*. Practicing the shakuhachi, a Japanese bamboo flute, inspires her poems. Poems from *Shadow of the Plum* may be heard on her CD, *Shadow of the Bamboo*, at www.carollem.com.

Sara Littlecrow-Russell, "Her Baskets," p. 76. *The Secret Powers of Naming* (University of Arizona Press, 2006) won Independent Publisher Book (Bronze), Gustavus Myers Outstanding Book (Center for the Study of Bigotry and Human Rights), *ForeWord Magazine* Book, and was a finalist in PEN/Beyond Margins.

Jeanne Lohmann, "Papyrus from an Egyptian Tomb," p. 38, lives and writes in Olympia, Washington. She is a graduate of the creative writing program at San Francisco State University. Her poems appear in many literary magazines and anthologies. *Calls From a Lighted House* is her eighth poetry collection.

Katharyn Howd Machan, "A Life," p. 55, professor of Writing and Women's Studies at Ithaca College, is the author of 28 published collections of poems, most recently *The Professor Poems* (Main Street Rag Publishing Company, 2008) and *Flags* (Pudding House Publications, 2007).

James A. McGrath, "A Space for Light," p. 52, "Sky of Reeds," p. 79, noted for his narrative poetry in the 1970's KAET/PBS American Indian Artist Series and two poetry collections with Sunstone Press, Santa Fe, New Mexico, he was USIS, Arts America, poet/artist-in-residence in Yemen, Saudi Arabia, and Republic of the Congo.

Robin Metz, "in double life," p. 12, Philip Sidney Post Professor of English and creative writing program director, has won distinguished teacher award and Rainer Maria Rilke International Poetry Prize. His poetry appears in collaboration with other arts and in *The Paris Review* and *International Poetry Review*.

Sheryl L. Nelms, "Rowing Across Wild Rice Lake," p. 78. Sheryl is from Marysville, Kansas. She graduated from SDSU. She has had over 4,500 articles, stories and poems published, including 11 collections of her work. She is currently the essay editor of *The Pen Woman Magazine*, the NLAPW publication.

Julia Older, "Cacoethes scribendi," pp. 39-40, has authored 25 books. Awarded the Daniel Varoujan Prize, Hopwood Poetry Award, Puffin Foundation, and Barbara Deming Memorial Fund grants, and an Iowa Poetry Workshop fellowship, her work appears in *Poets & Writers*, *The New Yorker*, *and Connecticut Review*.

Leonard Orr, "The Music We Play," p. 68, teaches literature at Washington State University. His work has appeared in many journals including *Black Warrior Review*, *Poetry International*, *Rosebud*, and *Poetry East*. His collection, *Why We Have Evening*, is forthcoming from Cherry Grove Editions.

Sherman Pearl, "Woodwinds," p. 84, winner of national and international poetry awards, co-founded the Los Angeles Poetry Festival and co-edits CQ (*California Quarterly*). His fifth poetry collection is *Profanities* (ConfluX Press, 2008). His poetry appears in literary journals and anthologies including *Poets Against the War*.

Robert Pinsky, "Ginza Samba," pp. 10-11, former U.S. Poet Laureate, literary critic, translator, editor, and columnist, has authored nineteen books. Awards include PEN/Voelcker, William Carlos Williams Prize, and Lenore Marshall, and is one of the few members of the American Academy of Arts and Letters to appear on *The Simpsons*.

Marianne Poloskey, "Rifles and Roses," p. 58. Her poetry has appeared in *The Christian Science Monitor*, *Connecticut Review*, *Louisiana Literature*, *Paterson Literary Review*, *The Spoon River Poetry Review*, *and Valparaiso Poetry Review*, among others. Her book *Climbing the Shadows* was published by Chi Chi Press, 2001.

Donna Pucciani, "Hautbois and the Night Visitors," p. 92, has published widely in the U.S. and U.K. Her books include *The Other Side of Thunder*, *Jumping Off the Train*, and *Chasing the Saints*. She is Vice President of Poets' Club of Chicago.

James Reiss, "Schilfgraben," p. 75. His honors include a Pushcart Prize, an NEA grant, and awards from Academy of American Poets and Poetry Society of America. Books include *Riff on Six: New and Selected Poems* (Salt Publishing, 2003), and poetry in *The New Yorker* and *The Paris Review*.

Francis L. Richardson, "The Instrument," p. 26, Professor Emeritus (Art History) at The Ohio State University, he is the author of *Andrea Schiavone* (Oxford University Press, USA, 1980), and a contributor to *Pavement Saw*, *Art Bulletin*, *The Burlington Magazine*, *Art Quarterly,* and other publications.

J.E. Robinson, "Miriam," p. 65, is an award-winning essayist, novelist, and poet whose work has appeared widely. He lives in southern Illinois, near St. Louis.

Levi Romero, "extranjero," pp.17-18, is from the Embudo valley of northern New Mexico. He is the author of *In the Gathering of Silence* and other publications. His latest poetry collection is *A Poetry of Remembrance: New and Rejected Works (*UNM Press, 2008).

Lynn Veach Sadler, "A Disquisition upon Thatch on the Way to Jane Austen's," pp. 80-81, former college president, editor, poet, playwright, and fiction/creative nonfiction writer, won *The Pittsburgh Quarterly*'s Hay Prize, *Kalliope*'s Elkind Contest, 2nd prize in *Spoon River Poetry Review* Editors' Prize contest, Poetry Society of America's Hemley Award, and *Asphodel*'s Poetry Contest.

Dennis Saleh, "Papyrus Wine," pp. 41-42, has published five books of poetry and edited an anthology of contemporary American poetry. His poems, prose, and artwork appear widely in the U.S. and overseas. He has read his work at the Rosicrucian Egyptian Museum in San Jose, California.

Kenneth Salzmann, "Paul Desmond's Last Date at Symphony Hall, Boston," p. 85, serves authors, publishers, and agents with Gelles-Cole Literary Enterprises, and is consultant to non-profit organizations throughout the country. His poems appear in *Rattle*, *Comstock Review*, *The Sow's Ear Poetry Review*, and *Perigee*.

Robert Samarotto, "Body and Soul," p. 95, professor of Music and Humanities, touring poet/musician member of Zeitgeist ensemble, received Jerome Foundation, NEA, and McKnight Foundation grants. His poems have appeared in *Ambergris*, *Buckle &*, *The Curbside Review*, *Milkweed Chronicle,* and *The Vegetable Book Project*.

Nancy Sather, "How We Came to Music," p. 59. Examples of poetry, reviews, short stories, and essays by Nancy Sather (MS Ecology, MFA Creative Writing), professional ecologist and freelance writer, can be found in *Appalachian Heritage, Water~Stone, Black Bear Review*, and Milkweed's *Stories from Where We Live*.

Sharon Scholl, "Electronic Clarinet: A Lament," p. 82, professor emeritus, held fellowships and grants from National Endowment for the Humanities, Woodrow Wilson Foundation, Witter Bynner Foundation (for a six-part TV series on local poetry venues and personalities), and authored *Unauthorized Biographies* and *All Points Bulletin* (Closet Books).

Maggie Smith, "Alum Creek, Late Summer," p. 20, "Gigging" p. 32, has two books, *Lamp of the Body* (Red Hen Press), Benjamin Saltman Poetry Award winner, and *Nesting Dolls* (Pudding House), Pudding House Chapbook Competition winner, and poems in *The Paris Review, The Gettysburg Review, Gulf Coast,* and *Indiana Review*.

Patricia Smith, "Map Rappin'," pp. 101-103, awarded International Literary Hall of Fame for Writers of African Descent, Best Poetry Book of 2006 (About.com), Hurston/Wright Legacy Award, Paterson Poetry Prize, National Book Award Finalist, and four national poetry slam championships, has authored five books of poetry.

Rick Smith, "To The Harmonica Players," pp. 29-31, a working harmonica player (see mescalsheiks.com for a sample), is a clinical psychologist, specializing in brain damage and domestic violence. *The Wren Notebook* (lummoxpress.com) is his most recent book. His poems appear in *Hunger Enough, Onthebus, Rattle,* and *New Letters*.

Rose M. Smith, "Roadside, Reeds," pp 36-37. Her work has appeared in just over a dozen journals, but she says her real joy is watching others achieve their publishing goals. She has served on editorial and special projects for Pudding House and facilitates the monthly Salon Columbus workshop series.

Spiel, "wetlands of lechwe," p. 13, "cattail club" p. 21. A Pushcart Prize contender, frequently published online and in independent press journals in multiple countries around the world, the poet Spiel creates diverse works of personal conflict and social consciousness. Learn more about his body of writings at: www.thepoetspiel.name.

Gina M. Tabasso, "Pathétique," p. 67, whose poems appear in many literary journals and in two chapbooks, *From Between My Legs* and *Disrobing*, works as a corporate communications manager and enjoys her horse, yoga, belly dancing, and being with those she loves.

Richard Terrill, "Five Reasons Not to Play the Tenor Saxophone," p. 90, Flight," pp. 98-99. He is the author of *Coming Late to Rachmaninoff* (poems) and two memoirs, including *Fakebook: Improvisations on a Journey Back to Jazz*. He teaches at Minnesota State University, Mankato, and works as a saxophone player in Minneapolis (http://english.mnsu.edu/terrill/).

Matthew Thorburn, "To an Oboe," p. 91, received a 2008 Witter Bynner Fellowship from the Library of Congress. He is the author of *Subject to Change* (New Issues, 2004) and a chapbook, *Disappears in the Rain* (Broome Review, 2009).

Nancy Wall, "Syrinx," p. 71, has lived in Tucson for most of her life and teaches at the University of Arizona and Pima Community College. Her book of poems *The Swiftness of Crows: Poems of Two Continents* was published by Moon Pony Press, 1999.

Sarah Brown Weitzman, "Yellow Corn Woman's Third Daughter," p. 77, grew up in Port Washington, NY, taught English at NYC, taught at NYU and recently retired to Delray Beach, Florida. Her third book of poetry, *Never Far From Flesh*, was published by Main Street Rag in 2005.

David Williams, "Listening to Coltrane's Blues," p. 100, has authored two poetry collections, *Traveling Mercies* (Alice James Books, 1993) and *Far Sides of the Only World* (Carolina Wren Press, 2004). His work appears in *The Atlantic*, *Hayden's Ferry Review*, *Kenyon Review*, and anthologies. He lives in Worcester, Massachusetts.

Carolyne Wright, "Last Dream in Perú," p. 33, won an Independent Book Publishers Bronze Award for *A Change of Maps* (Lost Horse Press, 2006), a Blue Lynx Prize, Oklahoma Book Award, American Book Award, PEN/Jerard Fund Award, Crossing Boundaries Award, Witter Bynner Foundation Grant, and numerous fellowships.

Kristin Camitta Zimet, "My Passover," p. 54, co-founded Appalachian Center for Poets and Writers and received a Poetry Society of America award. She was nominated for a Paterson Poetry Prize and Library of Virginia Literary Award for *Take in My Arms the Dark* (Sow's Ear Press, 1999).